Praise for

The Sinking of the SS Montebello

The Sinking of the SS Montebello *is the first time this fascinating narrative about a World War II enemy attack that touched the shores of the continental United States has been told. Kudos to author Stuart McDowell for tackling this story and bringing it to life.*

MIKE YORKEY

CO-AUTHOR OF "AT FIRST LIGHT," A WORLD WAR II STORY
OF STRUGGLES, SACRIFICES, AND SAVING THE LIPIZZANERS

This book is an extremely well written and fascinating account of a dramatic event that few citizens have ever heard of. There are many tales of heroism throughout World War II naval history, and this story is no exception.

JEFFREY NEVELS

CAPTAIN, U.S. NAVY (RET.)

Stuart McDowell melds the novelist's gift for storytelling with the historian's commitment to factual accuracy in his fast-paced, eloquently written The Sinking of the SS Montebello. *Readers are treated to a vivid historical overview of the events leading to World War II; the vital importance of oil transport ships during this era; civilian life along the California south-central coast before and after December 7, 1941; submarine warfare off the American West Coast after Pearl Harbor; all capped by a fascinating courtroom drama. This is a book for readers of history to savor and treasure."*

RICHARD KEZIRIAN

PROFESSOR EMERITUS, MONTEREY PENINSULA COLLEGE
AND PROFESSOR, THE PANETTA INSTITUTE FOR PUBLIC POLICY.

The sinking of one solitary ship brings into focus the conflict between nations and reveals struggles, still shared, over duty and integrity that will inspire debate among readers of all ages. McDowell paints a rich picture of history with the confluence of law, science, and environmentalism on the canvas of a world war fought, and largely forgotten, on the doorstep of California.

VICTOR PLATA

J.D., EDUCATOR, OLYMPIAN

... I found the McDowell book to be a delightful one-evening read. It is a page-turner, thanks to his forging of real history with a plot line worthy of Ken Follett and with the technical details of a Vince Flynn novel.

JOHN EHLERS

PAST PRESIDENT, CAMBRIA HISTORICAL SOCIETY

The Sinking
of the
SS Montebello

When World War II Came to the Central Coast of California

To my DEAR FRIEND, JIM FITZGERALD

I'LL ALWAYS BE THANKFUL FOR THE 10th
TEE AT PACIFIC GROVE!

Stuart McDowell

9/20/2021

Great Tidepool Press

Pacific Grove, California

Great Tidepool Press

Pacific Grove, California

Front cover: SS *Montebello* in Los Angeles Harbor. (Public domain.)

Cover designs by Bob Welch and Tom Penix.

All photos in the book without credits are public-domain images.

ISBN: 978-0-9772306-2-4

Author information: mcdowellsinpg@yahoo.com

For Sara McDowell Aycock,
my enthusiastic companion on father-daughter camping trips
to Morro Bay and San Simeon

Acknowledgments

The material for this project was gathered from many sources; the references included at the back of the book recognize them. My gratitude, however, extends further—to individuals who assisted in the process and who I want to thank specifically.

My thanks to:

Ryan Cooper and Jodie Nelson from the Piedras Blancas Light Station in San Simeon for their willing and helpful support during my visit there. They allowed me an opportunity to find the exact spot from which one character of the story, Norman Francis, observed the attack.

Tom Uretsky and his sister-in-law Polly Fry, who both assisted me in the project's research. Tom, a retired police detective, taught me basic computer investigative skills and provided early—and encouraging—information on Captain Olof Ekstrom.

Sgt. Maj. Daniel Sebby, Curator at the California Military Museum, for his generous permission to use images from the museum's archives, providing some of the best—and rarest—photos for the project.

Penny Church, for giving an informative tour of the Cambria Historical Museum when there were only two visitors—my wife, Caren, and me. It was there we saw the oar from the *Montebello*. Penny's love for Cambria and its history was infectious.

Kaylee Scoggins Herring, Collection Manager of the Historical Center of San Luis Obispo County, for her diligent searching of the archives for specific images I requested and to the Historical Center for permission to use them.

Mark Cameron, for sharing his expertise as a trial attorney in viewing the *Montebello* court documents and providing insight into the legal process and strategies of the plaintiff's and defendant's lawyers.

Vic Hansen, for his kind and quick permission to use the *Alma* photo with Montebello survivors. And to Robert Sanchez, Connie Sanchez, Jeff Nevels, Victor Plata, and Kathy Buller, who all, along with Mark, read the manuscript and offered suggestions. And to Bill Winchester, who patiently listened to my many retellings of stories related to the *Montebello* and responded with encouraging feedback.

Dr. Richard Kezirian provided the scrutiny of a college history professor while reviewing the manuscript and offered valued historical perspectives and suggestions.

To my editor, Bob Welch, I am particularly indebted. His editing, focus, guidance, and encouragement was essential to my progress. And he managed to provide it all while fostering a sense of teamwork. Without him, I would not have thought it feasible to begin this project in the first place.

Finally, I wish to express undying appreciation to my wife of forty years, Caren. She read each chapter numerous times, considered every photograph, and gave me the measured and tactful input she knew I required—and always in a manner I could receive it. One must understand a person very well to consistently accomplish that. Caren listened with extraordinary patience to the details and characters of this story and reacted with an enthusiasm that helped fuel my resolve. For that—and so very much more—I will always be grateful.

Contents

Author's Note

During my lifetime, I've heard stories that caught my attention and would not let go. The SS *Montebello* is one of them. I first learned of the ship as a young boy while living by the Pacific Ocean in Southern California. Each year, my family would vacation in Morro Bay on the Central Coast. It was there, in the mid-1960s, that I heard of the *Montebello* being attacked by a Japanese submarine at the beginning of World War II.

Although my family had lived in California for generations, none of my relatives were aware of the incident. My parents and I learned together from the scant bits of information available at the time. On library visits during my twenties, I occasionally ran across a document, a casualty report, or a customs officer's letter regarding the oil tanker. I imagined a day when I would find a book that told the whole story. But over years of searching, I discovered no such book.

One day in 1995, I was at the National Archives branch in San Bruno doing ancestry research. A few hours before closing, I asked if, by chance, the archives had a file on the *Montebello*. Soon, the assistant librarian placed before me a paper-thin folder containing a handful of documents, all of which I'd seen before.

"I thought the file would be much larger," I said.

The young woman's eyebrows raised. "Oh, do you want to see the folder of the trial?"

Trial?

Minutes later, she returned with a file four inches thick. As I turned the pages, I realized herein lay many of the details of the fascinating story of the *Montebello* and the ship's intriguing fate.

As years passed, I fully expected to see a book offering a comprehensive rendition of the ship's story. But in my searches, I still hadn't found one. I finally asked myself if the story I wished to read surrounding the Montebello had not yet been written, why not write it myself?

My years of research resulted in something resembling a large jigsaw puzzle, hundreds of pieces of information strewn about that needed proper placement to form a clear picture of what happened that day in December 1941. Often, I found answering one question led to a handful more. But I was committed to telling as full a story as I could, so tried to answer them all.

Are there more details of the ship's history still hiding somewhere? Surely. However, in *The Sinking of the* SS *Montebello,* I've aspired to blend the most important elements of the vessel, the outcome, the place, the time, and the characters involved into an accurate telling of this little-known story whose centerpiece lies ghost-like in the waters off California's Central Coast.

Stuart McDowell
Pacific Grove, California
August 2021

Prologue

As he stood atop the submarine's conning tower, the sight and scent of the previous spring's cherry blossoms back home were far behind Kanji Matsumura. Instead, the thoughts of the Imperial Japanese Navy commander were focused on a target in the distance: a U.S. tanker easing its way north of Morro Bay on the Central California coast.

The prey.

It was December 23, 1941, sixteen days after the Japanese attack on Hawaii's Pearl Harbor. In the inky, pre-dawn darkness, Matsumura and his deck officers peered through their waterproof binoculars. They could see the faint wake of the tanker ahead of them.

Matsumura's sub was impressive in size—longer than a football field. And fast. He would be able to close the gap on the tanker easily. It was still ninety minutes before first light, just before 5 AM. He wanted to execute the attack before the sun rose and American air patrols could be summoned. The commander had ample time to find what he was looking for—what submariners referred to as "a favorable attack position."

Along with the cherry blossoms, behind Matsumura, too, were the pleasant summer days spent outfitting his 356-foot Imperial Japanese Navy submarine, the *I-21*. Only two weeks before, he and his crew had been in Hawaiian waters and able to pick up radio broadcasts from Honolulu. The "sounds of aloha" music drifted through the submarine's compartments, as if played on a scratchy phonograph record at the Island's radio station. The carefree melodies of a ukulele had only strengthened the confidence of each man aboard. The attack planned for December 7, Hawaiian time, was, as they'd hoped, completely unexpected; the Americans were awash in blissful ignorance.

The enormous success of the lightning strike at Pearl Harbor seemed both a triumphant, yet distant, memory. The *I-21* was in California waters now. And Matsumura's mindset was determined and precise. He had seventeen torpedoes aboard and a strict limit of one per merchant target—the exception being a U.S. Navy vessel. In such cases, all limits were off. He'd have one shot on this morning; this was not a military vessel. And if it were well placed, one shot would be all he'd need.

The target, the SS *Montebello,* belonged to the Union Oil fleet. The previous day, the tanker had finished being loaded with more than three-million gallons of crude oil. She was traveling without escort. While Atlantic Ocean merchant ships commonly had some measure of protective accompaniment against German U-boats, such was not the case on the West Coast sea lanes. Though that scenario would change within a few months, in December 1941 merchant ships lacked even a deck gun. The only weapon the ship's captain had was a single pistol; in other words, the *Montebello* was utterly defenseless.

But American concerns of West Coast attacks had spiraled within the previous five days. Japanese submarines had fired upon at least four merchant ships off the coast. Further, the attack on Hawaii had raised worry about Japan's capacity for aerial attacks on the U.S. mainland itself; the annual Rose Bowl football game had already been moved from Pasadena, California, to Durham, North Carolina. Coastal beach patrols had been quickly established all along Washington, Oregon, and California. Night blackouts, including car headlights, were being enforced. The potential of attack was real, and along the West Coast, in every citizen's thoughts.

Certainly, aboard the *Montebello* early that morning, the crew was on high-alert. Each man's anxiety heightened even more when, suddenly, they heard thunderous explosions from an attack several miles behind them—on another ship, they quickly discovered. Now, the captain and crew knew an enemy raider was in the area. Like hunted prey running through a dark forest, stalked by an unseen pursuer, the ship and her crew of thirty-seven plied forward in the choppy seas with a mix of dread and hope.

Perhaps the fifteen miles they'd traveled since the explosions were enough. Perhaps they'd passed through the sector unnoticed by the submarine. Then again, perhaps not.

"Life jackets on!" came the command from the communication tube.

Lookouts had been posted and lights snuffed. Among the crew, throats tightened, hearts quickened.

The *Montebello* was several miles west of the beaches of Cambria and a similar distance south of the lighthouse at Piedras Blancas near San Simeon. Rain fell in thin sheets, starting, stopping, and starting again.

Back on the sub, Matsumura and other officers leaned forward on the top of the conning tower, knowing that if they followed the wake carefully they would eventually find the ship. Below, within the body of the submarine, the *I-21's* crew awaited each order for bearing and speed—responding with quick efficiency. The diesel engines, used when running on the surface, purred, but also contributed to the distinctive smell that permeated every compartment of the boat. "Submarine perfume" was a damp mix of sweat, condensation, the last cooked meal, and diesel. Always diesel.

The conning tower was amid ship and easily had space for six officers. It gave the best perch for surface navigation, signaling, and a comprehensive field of view. But the tower also rose nearly eighteen-feet in height above the deck making it the most visible part of the submarine from a distance. The boat's stealth lay below the waterline. Even so, a submarine had to exercise extreme diligence in searching the skies for signs of air patrols—with hopes of spotting them at such distances that they'd have time to make an emergency dive. From the air, and with the light of day, a submarine was still visible up to fifty feet below the ocean surface. Depth bombs dropped on a visually confirmed target were lethal.

Matsumura called for an increase in speed.

Near 5:15 AM, the wake of the *Montebello*—a bubbled and swirling trail stretching for miles—grew more defined ahead of the submarine's bow; running on the surface, the sub was creeping closer. Gradually, the black silhouette of the tanker came into the commander's view; he was directly astern of his target now and lowered his speed to maintain the gap between vessels. It was time to find his "favorable point of attack."

The *Montebello's* lookouts had spotted something behind the ship. Like Matsumura, its captain and crew, too, could see a silhouette—the *I-21's* conning tower—about a mile astern. The captain ran to the bridge wing, looked aft, and ordered the helmsman, "Hard right rudder!" The sluggish tanker, riding low in the water with her holds full of explosive cargo, slowly began to swing to starboard. Coming out of the turn, the helmsman straightened her for a minute or two before the next order came. "Hard left!"

A zigzagging target would be more difficult, more challenging, in producing the precise calculations required for the submarine's attack. At least, that was the captain's hope. But Matsumura had ordered more speed and shifted his position to starboard, placing the *I-21* between the mainland and the *Montebello*. Aboard the tanker, the officers watched as the submarine quickly reduced the mile gap and the boat altered its position. From the bridge wing, they could still identify the sub's black conning tower. Then the silhouette slowly shrank and disappeared. She was going stealth,

Matsumura, com-
mander of the I-21.

beneath the sea.

Matsumura and his officers descended from the open bridge atop the conn, into the enclosed control room, and ordered the boat submerge to periscope depth. The electric engines were engaged and diesel engines shut down. Through the periscope, Matsumura tracked the distance and movements of the *Montebello* and repositioned the boat to what he'd waited for all along—the favorable attack position. He was now in a textbook position to fire—approximately nine hundred-yards from the *Montebello*. Matsumura called the torpedo control room and gave the order to arm and load the torpedo.[1]

Hunched over the periscope handles, the commander now ordered the torpedo tube flooded and gathered final numbers for speed, bearing, and range. As the oil tanker began to emerge from another hard right turn, Matsumura ordered the tube's muzzle door opened, and waited. The *I-21* slowly reached a ninety-degree angle to the target's path. The commander gave the order. "Fire!"

The fire control technician raised the red cover that must be lifted to access the firing switch—the last safety measure after the weapon has been armed—and launched the torpedo. A burst of compressed air and a hydraulic push of water expelled the weapon, over twenty-three feet in length, from the tube.

The torpedo sped forward like a horse from the gate. It had duel four-blade propellers, one spinning clockwise and the other counter-clockwise, and was powered by compressed oxygen. As the bomb accelerated to a speed of fifty miles per hour, Matsumura knew the weapon should reach the *Montebello* in about forty seconds. The impact would propel a firing pin into the 893-pound warhead. The commander fixed his gaze upon his stopwatch, counting the seconds, and waited for the victorious sound of detonation.

Chapter One

The Montebello

At Terminal Island in San Pedro, California, the Southwestern Shipbuilding Company was a cacophony of sounds. Grinders whirled, welding torches popped, and huge cranes groaned under their loads. Plumbers, riveters, electricians, riggers, carpenters, and steel workers created their own distinct noise. And to the builders who worked with steel beams and plates to create the ships that went to sea, there was a beauty to it.

It was at Southwestern, in 1920, that the Union Oil company placed an order for two tankers. The two vessels would be named the *Montebello* and the *La Placentia*—her sister ship. They would be the petroleum corporation's new method of mass transport.

It hadn't taken long for Union Oil to figure it out. The company could transport oil farther, faster, and in much greater quantities if they moved it in large shipping vessels instead of on trains and trucks.

On April 20, 1920, the keel was laid for both ships at Southwestern. Only nine months later, on January 24, 1921, the *Montebello* was launched. A company crowd gathered for the ceremony where Miss Adelaide Stewart, daughter of Union Oil Company

The *SS Montebello* launching at Southwestern Shipbuilding Company
in San Pedro, California, January 24, 1921.

president William Stewart, acted as sponsor, christening her "SS
Montebello " in honor of the productive nearby oil fields of the
same name. Both the *Montebello* and the *La Placentia*, huge for
their time, were 440-feet in length and 58 feet abeam. Both vessels were steel-hulled with double bottoms.

A 3,300-horsepower vertical reciprocating steam engine—coupled with a single screw propeller—would generate propulsion;
the combination was able to produce eleven knots of speed. Her
cargo space, capable of carrying 94,000 barrels of oil, was divided
into eighteen main tanks, nine on each side, and ten "summer
tanks" (commonly used to move water ballast during the loading
of cargo to maintain proper trim).

The tanker's outfitting and sea trials were completed successfully
by March 2, 1921. Eight days later, the *Montebello* arrived at Port
San Luis—an important oil shipping and storage facility of Union
Oil. The vessel made her maiden voyage on March 12, carrying
81,000 barrels of oil from Port San Luis to Union Oil's Oleum

storage and refinery facilities on San Pablo Bay in San Francisco.[2] She returned to Port San Luis, loaded another 81,000 barrels into her holds, and completed a more lengthy delivery, this time to Vancouver, British Columbia—the first of hundreds of trips the ship would make to Vancouver during her twenty-year career.

The company magazine, the *Union Oil Bulletin*, described their deep-sea fleet in a 1933 article.

> The white 'U' on the black stacks of the trim-hulled tankers of the Union Oil Company's deep sea fleet has become a familiar sight to the mariners plying the trade lanes of the Pacific and Atlantic during the past twenty-five years. Tireless carriers—these vessels transporting California oil products to the far-flung ports of the Western Hemisphere. They are here today and gone tomorrow.
>
> There are no long delays in their home ports where they load cargoes and clear in from eight to twenty-four hours. This is made possible by the perfection of machinery and loading methods and cooperation between dock and ship crews. As a result, the tankers spend only about four percent of their time in port. The rest of the time they are out at sea.
>
> Since 1930, Union Oil tankers have at various times gone as far north as Nome, Alaska, and south as far as around the Horn

The *Montebello* resting well above water with her storage tanks empty.
The "U" on the funnel identified it as a Union Oil vessel.

and up to Buenos Aires. They have been west as far as Hankow and Shanghai, China, and east as far as Montreal, Canada, Rotterdam, and Hamburg.

The *Montebello* was almost exclusively a Pacific Ocean tanker. There were exceptions. She made several voyages through the Panama Canal Zone to the East Coast of the United States, but those destinations were rare. Other voyages saw the *Montebello* travel to Puerto Lobos (Mexico), Balboa in the Panama Canal Zone, or the Chilean ports of Iquique, Antofagasta, and Taltal.

Still other circumstances required the vessel to engage in long-haul operations delivering oil products to ports along the eastern Pacific and to Honolulu. For a five-year period beginning in 1926, she made a number of deliveries to the Panama Canal and Chile. Then slowly, her primary sea-routes shifted back to the North American West Coast.

Occasionally, routine operations on the tanker were interrupted to assist another ship, transfer an ailing crewmember for medical assistance, or even to witness a natural phenomenon. In early January of 1926, while returning from a Chilean oil delivery, the *Montebello* crew observed a rare sight: Albemarle Island, of the Galapagos group, was birthing a new volcano.

The *Honolulu Star-Bulletin* published a brief story of the event. "The discovery was reported by Capt. J.S. Collier of the Union Oil tanker *Montebello*, which sighted the volcano January 5. The tanker approached within a half-mile of the island and took photographs which revealed a small crater about a half-mile inland ... lava was pouring forth in a stream twenty-feet wide into the ocean, where the contact of the lava with the water created vapor which partly obscured, in the photographs, the details of the fissure."

Charles Darwin, the article noted, had once written, "It would be difficult to find in any other part of the world an island situated within the tropics and of such considerable size (seventy-five miles long) so sterile and incapable of supporting life." Despite the forbidding nature of the place, said the *Star-Bulletin*, "the islands have been inhabited at times. Charles Island was once a frequent resort of pirates, and a penal colony was established there by the Ecuadorian government."

In November 1940, the ship was chartered—for one trip—by Ioco (Imperial Oil Corporation) to carry oil between Peru and Vancouver to the company's facilities at Port Moody, the *Montebello's* most frequent off-loading location, either at the Union Oil or Ioco docks. The tanker also made occasional calls at Esquimalt, near Victoria, on the southern tip of Vancouver Island.

On September 6, 1941, the *Montebello* sailed for the U.S.S.R. to deliver fuel. While at port in Siberia, a light-hearted moment occurred—with the cooperation of Captain Mogens Andreasen and First Mate Olof Ekstrom. A trans-Pacific birthday message was sent. A member of the ship's crew radioed the greetings to his father in St. Louis Park, Minnesota. The *Minneapolis Star* reported, "Birthday greetings radioed from Siberia were received by Walter Thomas, 4073 Alabama Avenue, St. Louis Park, on his seventieth birthday. The message, 'Seventieth Anniversary Greetings' was sent by his son, Gordon Thomas, thirty-three, now chief steward aboard the SS *Montebello,* [the] tanker which delivered the first

The *Montebello*, fully loaded, passing through Burrard Inlet, Vancouver, B.C. on her way to Port Moody. (*Vancouver Maritime Museum*)

big shipment of United States oil to Russia in September." Such carefree moments would soon become the exception rather than the rule.

War was escalating in Europe and the Far East, threatening to engulf the United States in both theaters. Late in 1941, the U.S. Navy had directed merchant vessels to participate in degaussing and calibration.

This was a technique for protecting ships from mine explosions. British scientists had discovered a ship wasn't required to have direct contact with a German mine for it to explode. The mine, they found, was detonated by the magnetic signature of a ship passing close by. The solution was to reduce the magnetic signature by hanging a copper cable along the ship's side and then passing an electrical current through it, a process called "degaussing."

In the National Archives quarterly *Prologue*, Suzanne Dewberry's article, "Perils at Sea," described how merchant vessels were

The *Montebello* at dry dock in San Francisco. The size of the ship is evident in contrast to the worker visible left of the propeller, by the ladders.
(San Francisco Maritime National Park)

to be scheduled for such modifications. "On August 13, 1941, the Union Oil Company, owners of the *Montebello*, informed the Navy that the ship was due for a short overhaul at the Los Angeles Shipbuilding and Drydock Company and would be available for degaussing."

"The Navy," Dewberry said, "responded that in order for degaussing to take place, sufficient materials had to be delivered to San Pedro. It is not clear from the records whether the degaussing actually took place during the overhaul before the next scheduled voyage."

The *Montebello* did receive the minor overhaul. Along with repairs, the tanker was given a new coat of paint—all gray—in preparation for the likelihood of war. The Navy called it "haze gray," the war paint used to make ships tougher to see. Even the Queen Mary was given a new coat of the paint, leading to her nickname "The Gray Ghost" during her war service as a troop ship.

After the December 7, 1941, Pearl Harbor attack, the oil industry recognized the government's claim upon oil products the industry could produce as the country's attitude shifted—within a day—to an all-out war effort. Reese Taylor, president of Union Oil at the time, said, "So long as the war lasts, supplying government needs must be the company's first responsibility." In the war effort to which the nation was now committed, the oil industry was tasked with the responsibility of providing the enormous amounts of petroleum the armed services would need.

Map of San Luis Obispo County 1940

Chapter Two

Home Port

The agreeable rush-and-drag sound of small waves breaking along the shore was ever-present at Port San Luis. So was the stubborn scent of crude oil in the town of Avila. The *Montebello* was familiar with both whenever she entered the port.

On the ship's transom, the city of Los Angeles was emblazoned as the SS *Montebello's* official home. But it was home in name only. The tanker made far and away more visits to-and-from the port at San Luis. The loading facility here was the starting point for the *Montebello* on hundreds of voyages. Ship and crew always considered Port San Luis and the little township of Avila—less than a half-mile walk from the Union Oil pier—to be home.

Avila had little to brag about beyond oil and the port. The 1942 *Coast Pilot* referred to the town as "a small settlement of no commercial importance." The community was indeed small, but also close-knit and hard-working. Avila was not the wingtips-and-ties look of workers in downtown Los Angeles; if you weren't an oil worker you were a fisherman. And if you weren't one of those two you were a station-hand with the railroad, a rancher, farmer, waitress, café owner, or a service station operator—the kind who

Port San Luis during the SS *Montebello's* era. The Union Oil pier is visible in the center; the town of Avila can be seen in the lower right.
(History Center of San Luis Obispo County)

checked your oil *and* washed your windows.

The hilltops above Avila were lined with oil storage tanks. Below in the bay, small fishing boats sprinkled the surface of the water. The town had built a two-room schoolhouse in 1913 to replace the tiny one-room school constructed ten years earlier.

But the heartbeat of Avila was Front Street, which ran parallel and adjacent to the beach. There, among the most notable establishments in the early '40s was a saloon, the New Moon Inn, a burger joint, the Avila Fountain, and, the social center of town, the Avila Grocery. All were located a kicked-can distance from the pier and popular with both the local citizens and the merchant seamen of the *Montebello* when the ship was in port.

While the New Moon specialized in beer and hard liquor, the Avila Fountain served Pepsi-Cola, Nesbitt's Orange Soda, and 7-Up—along with burgers and shakes. Everything else could be found at the Avila Grocery—and if they didn't have it, they'd find a way to get it.

Avila Grocery carried everything, including Union Gasoline.

Although Avila began as a nondescript oil port, that was about to change. In 1927, with the increased commerce produced by oil exports there, the federal government had decided the need existed to build a Customs House in town—across the vacant lot south of the grocery—to manage the entrance and clearance of vessels at Port San Luis.

The building was dedicated on March 19 and the event was a

Avila's U.S. Custom House was dedicated March 19, 1927.
(History Center of San Luis Obispo County)

spectacle even by today's standards. Approximately 3,500 people arrived in little Avila that Saturday, "bathed in golden sunshine," as the *Fresno Morning Republican* wrote. There were flags, a parade of decorated automobiles through town, and a band that played the national anthem. There were Coast Guard vessels and yacht club boats in the bay, a luncheon, commercial leaders from Los Angeles to San Francisco, and speakers—including U.S. Sen. Samuel Southridge, who gave a rousing pledge to provide every federal assistance that could aid the port.

The *Montebello's* reason for being in Port San Luis was singular—oil. The port itself had grown in importance after oil was discovered in Kern County in the San Joaquin Valley.[3]

In 1909, Union Oil Company of California, along with several other outfits, began laying over two hundred miles of pipeline from the oil fields there to the storage facilities in San Luis Obispo and Avila, which together possessed a stockpile capacity of twenty-seven million barrels. Prior to the exporting of "black gold," the tiny seaside settlement of Avila, tucked into the southeastern cusp of the bay, had been considered an insignificant collection of shacks. That would change quickly; in less than a year, the first oil from the Kern River fields reached Port San Luis.

Over a forty-year period, there had been three piers constructed in the bay. The Harford Wharf, built in 1873, was the first of importance. The wharf was at the north corner of the bay near the breakwater. The wharf itself was later extended, and, for a time, accommodated the small oil tankers of the era.

About one and one-half miles southeast of Harford Wharf was Avila Pier, initially built in 1908. County Wharf—as it was called in 1941—extended to a depth of twenty-five feet and was utilized primarily by fishing and pleasure boats.

Within a short time, Union Oil became the sole owner of the oil pipeline to the storage tanks at Avila but lacked any efficient means of dispensing the oil. Recognizing the need, the Pacific Coast Railway Company began construction of a third pier in 1914—located roughly halfway between the two existing wharfs—specifically for the commercial shipping of oil. Union Oil immediately contracted to lease the new pier. Within a decade, use of Harford Wharf for the shipment of oil had ceased.

Thereafter, all oil was loaded from Pier No. 2, which by now was owned by Union Oil. Known as "Middle Dock," the pier extended into the bay 3,150-feet. At the outer end, ships had a depth of thirty feet at low tide. Oil tankers—the only deep-draft vessels to now enter the bay—used Middle Dock to load cargos of oil. Shipments of petroleum products, by this time, made up 99 percent of the commercial traffic of the port.

In 1941, Port San Luis remained a principle terminal for the Union Oil Company. Like the locomotive trains that migrated from one freight hub to another, oil tankers sailed a never-ending series of load and discharge voyages along the coast. Ships frequented the facilities at Port San Luis and Estero Bay—a few miles north of Morro Rock. At both sites, vessels loaded with bows facing seaward in the direction of the prevailing northwesterly winds. Standard Oil Tankers docked at the facilities at the Estero pier. But Union Oil tankers used Port San Luis and the *Montebello* lived at Middle Dock in the center of the crescent shaped bay off Avila.

The ship was considered a "shelter deck" tanker and big for its day. Between the main tanks and summer tanks of the ship, the vessel could handle slightly more than 82,000 barrels, equal in volume to six Olympic-size swimming pools.

Such an enormous amount of oil took considerable time to load—twenty-four hours, to be precise. Pipelines streamed down from the storage tanks above Avila to the pier at Middle Dock. Along the left and right sides of the pier, pipes were fitted to relay different grades of crude oil to the vessels awaiting their consignment.

The *Montebello* typically carried a crew of thirty-eight men. Her voyages along the Pacific Coast were frequently of two- or three-day duration. With generally a one-day intermission to unload at locations such as Oleum, Victoria, or Vancouver, the ship would then make the quick turn-around and return home to Port San

Luis—to refill yet again. There were, of course, exceptions—such as the voyages to South America or elsewhere. But the northwest corridor to these ports-of-call was the bread-and-butter of the *Montebello's* workload.

The tanker's re-entry into the bay at San Luis was always a welcome and pleasant homecoming. The vessel would pass Point Buchon on her port side, then the lighthouse above the port, and finally the breakwater. Once secured at Middle Dock, the crew would hustle into Avila and, depending on the inclination of the moment, head to the New Moon Inn or the Fountain.

Chapter Three

Matsumura and the Rising Sun

It was an ancient province, the Yamaguchi Prefecture on the island of Honshu. During the rise of the samurai class—beginning in 794 A.D.—powerful warrior clans existed here. By the time Kanji Matsumura was born in 1899, the days of shoguns and samurai had been replaced by a modern government—with modern goals for industry and agriculture.

There had been a shipbuilding plant in Yamaguchi and it was perhaps the influence of the harbors and vessels around him that ignited a young Matsumura's interest in naval service. At age eighteen, he left the prefect to enroll in the prestigious Imperial Japanese Naval Academy.

The academy had been previously based in Tokyo but was relocated in 1888 to Etajima, a beautiful Y-shaped island in Hiroshima Bay. Here, candidates who successfully completed four years of studies graduated with the commission of midshipman. At age twenty-two, Matsumura became a member of the academy's fiftieth graduating class.

He was assigned for sea duty upon the 400-foot armored cruiser *Izumo*. Eight months later, he would be transferred to the

Honso, the Imperial Navy's first aircraft carrier, and soon promoted to Ensign.

But Matsumura was destined for submarines. He returned to school for gunnery and torpedo training, rose to the rank of Lieutenant, and in 1928, joined the crew of the *I-54*. Matsumura would remain in the submarine service the rest of his naval career.

By late 1935, he had achieved the rank of Lieutenant Commander—and again participated in advanced submarine training. At each stage, Matsumura displayed promise and was rewarded with improving assignments. As the fall of 1941 approached, he received yet another coveted promotion—to Commander. On the last day of October, Matsumura was named skipper of the new submarine, the *I-21*.

Japan had begun developing submarines in earnest shortly after their war with Russia in 1905. By 1941 and the initiation of war with America, the Empire's navy had a fleet of sixty-five submarines, nearly three times as many as the United States' Pacific Fleet (twenty-three).

Japan's Type B-1 submarine was the initial group of new boats developed. The first of these was the *I-15*, which gave the alternate name of "I-Class" to the series. These submarines represented impressive advances in both design and engineering.

Work on the *I-21* began at the Kawasaki Shipyard, Kobe, in January 1939. Thirteen months later she was launched, then outfitted, and ready for sea trials by July 1941. The boat was fast—capable of twenty-four knots on the surface—and big. She

Type B-1 *I-15* during sea trails in 1940. The boat was the same model as the *I-21*. Curved floatplane hangar and catapult are visible.

measured 356 feet in length, 30.5 feet abeam, and was tested to depths of 330 feet.

The submarine was powered by diesel and electric motors and possessed a cruising range of 14,000 miles before needing to refuel—ideal for action in the wide Pacific Ocean. Diesel motors were used for surface cruising while the quiet electric motors were utilized underwater, producing speeds up to eight knots.

The *I-21* was manned by a compliment of ninety-four officers and crew. Her armament was formidable. She carried seventeen Type-95 torpedoes that could be fired from six tubes—three each on the port and starboard sides of the submarine's bow. Each devastating torpedo weighed more than 3,600 pounds, carried a huge 893-pound explosive charge, and had an impressive range of 12,000 meters.

For surface action, the boat was also armed with a five-inch "deck gun" aft of the conning tower—firing projectiles that packed an explosive wallop.

Finally, tucked inside a waterproof tube-like hanger was one Yokosuka "Glen" floatplane—launched by catapult—giving the commander "beyond horizon" reconnaissance capabilities. In short, the *I-21* possessed long range capabilities and weaponry that presented a significant threat to American navy and merchant vessels.

On November 10, 1941, only ten days after Kanji Matsumura was assigned commanding officer, Vice-Admiral Mitsumi Shimizu assembled a meeting of his submarine commanders aboard his flagship, the light cruiser *Katori*, to receive a briefing of the planned attack on Pearl Harbor.

By November 19, the *I-21* had sailed from Yokosuka to rendezvous at the assembly point for the strike force at Etorofu Island—a location chosen for its isolation. The force sailed from there on November 26 with commanders knowing the fleet may be recalled if negotiations taking place in Washington D.C. yielded a favorable outcome. Meanwhile, Japan's fleet steamed toward a point 275 miles north of the Hawaiian island of Oahu.

Those negotiations were part of the ongoing tensions between the United States and the Empire of Japan, stressors that were now at a breaking point. For nearly a decade, the Japanese had embarked on a campaign of military expansion with barbaric invasions of both mainland China and French-Indochina. In protest, America began to tighten restrictions on Japan.

The United States was the main supplier of oil, steel, and other commodities needed by the Japanese military. The U.S. government increasingly enforced an embargo of needed resources against Japan in an effort to persuade the Empire to withdraw from the invaded territories. Such an outcome was unacceptable to Japanese military leaders.

By November 1941, Japan was faced with serious shortages as a result of the embargo. Moreover, they believed that U.S. officials would oppose any further negotiations. If such a scenario proved true, Japan's leaders had concluded that they had to act swiftly with a military strike.

Indeed, all further attempts of negotiation failed. On December 2, the strike force received the coded signal "Climb Mount Niitaka," indicating that hostilities would commence on December 8 (Japan time). In the Hawaiian Islands, however, the calendar would read December 7, "a date which will live in infamy" as President Franklin Roosevelt declared before a joint session of the U.S. Congress the following day.

Nine I-Class Japanese submarines, including the *I-21*, were assigned to provide fleet protection. The boats established a picket-line 120 miles north of Oahu—between the island and the fleet—the morning of the attack. The *I-21* had begun its first war patrol.

The initial wave of Japanese torpedo planes appeared over Pearl Harbor at 7:53 AM and dive-bombers soon followed. The second wave of the attack arrived at 8:40 AM. It was over in less than two hours. Japanese forces had unleashed a devastating assault on the naval base at Pearl Harbor and the military airfields across Hawaii.

With much of the U.S. Pacific Fleet now in ruins—and 2,334 U.S. military personnel dead—the Imperial Japanese Navy retired

Honolulu Star-Bulletin 1st EXTRA

6 PAGES—HONOLULU, TERRITORY OF HAWAII, U. S. A., SUNDAY, DECEMBER 7, 1941—3 PAGES ★ PRICE FIVE CENTS

WAR !

(Associated Press by Transpacific Telephone)

SAN FRANCISCO, Dec. 7.—President Roosevelt announced this morning that Japanese planes had attacked Manila and Pearl Harbor.

OAHU BOMBED BY JAPANESE PLANES

Before December 7, 1941 was over, the *Honolulu Star-Bulletin*
had reported news of the attack that drew the United States into World War II.

from the theater of battle, set course, and returned to the Empire's home waters.

But not all of the fleet would follow. Nine submarines—the *I-21* among them—were ordered to proceed to the West Coast of the United States and attack American merchant shipping—and any U.S. Navy ships sighted. The intention of the Japanese strategy was twofold: First, Japan hoped to prevent any naval reinforcement of Hawaii from the mainland of the United States. Second, the attacks were intended to create a fear of invasion in the population and spread panic among Americans, thereby forcing the U.S. to commit significant military resources to defending the entire coastal homeland. That, of course, would mean the U.S. would have fewer resources to use when fighting Japan elsewhere in the world.

Commander Matsumura and the *I-21* were assigned to patrol the waters off Point Arguello, California, an exiled point of land that, despite its isolation, saw frequent coastal shipping pass by. This would place the IJN submarine only forty nautical miles south of Port San Luis.

Now in position to attack the sea lanes off the coast, Matsumura and his crew waited and watched. They would soon find the
prey they were seeking. In the early morning hours of December
23, 1941, the submarine would attack two oil tankers before the
first rays of sunlight touched the waters off the Central Coast.

The Imperial Japanese Naval Academy in Etajima, Hiroshima.

Chapter Four

Captains of the Montebello

Two names are most remembered in association with the SS *Montebello*. Both men were foreign born and both competent shipmasters. Mogens Andreasen had captained the tanker on many occasions during his career, but his name is most often recalled as the master who completed the *Montebello's* final successful voyage—and the master who did not sail her last.

Andreasen had been born in Denmark in 1881. It was a period of industrial awakening in the country; the first railways had been constructed and overseas trade markets increased. None of that interested Andreasen more than the sea. He began his career working aboard ships at sixteen years of age.

Andreasen's focus was apparently never far away from "Amerika." In 1908, an opportunity to immigrate to the United States came, and he took it. By 1912, he had become a naturalized citizen in a ceremony where he would renounce all loyalties to King Frederick VIII of Denmark.

The following year, Andreasen moved to San Francisco and was hired by the Union Oil Company of California. Not physically imposing—Mogens stood only 5 feet 8 inches tall and weighed

Captain Mogens Andreasen

155 pounds—the thirty-two-year-old sailor exuded an air of command and competence, reaching the position of Master in a mere three and a half years.

In 1929, the *Union Oil Bulletin* provided a brief summary of the Danish master's ascension. "Captain Mogens Andreasen, now in command of the twin-screw Union Oil tanker SS *Oleum*, joined the company's fleet March 4, 1913, as third mate of the SS *Whittier*. He was raised through the ranks and appointed Master of the *Whittier* in August 1916. He has served as master aboard a number of ships in the company's deep-sea fleet."

Andreasen was appointed Captain of the SS *Montebello* in 1933. As a general rule, his assignments were transporting oil from Port San Luis to the Union Oil facilities in Vancouver, British Columbia. Occasionally, however, the company engaged in contracts that took Andreasen and his ship to South America. In 1927, he captained the *Oleum* to Manzanillo, Mexico. In 1929, he guided the *Montebello* to Iquique, Chile, then in 1930 to the Canal Zone, and in 1940 to Antofagasta, Chile.

In September 1941, Andreasen accepted the role serving as master on a voyage of greater urgency and concern. The United States Maritime Commission had granted approval to the Union Oil Company to charter the *Montebello* to the Amtorg Trading Company, an agency of the Soviet government. The Soviet Union had been invaded by Nazi Germany in June 1941. Badly in need of oil, the Soviet government—with the blessing of the U.S. Maritime Commission—chartered the *Montebello* to deliver a full load of crude to the Russian port at Magadan.

The ship and crew of the *Montebello* would have to pass north of the Japanese Empire's home islands to reach the port on the Sea of Okhotsk.

Andreasen charted a course that took the tanker across the North Pacific, then through the Kuril Straits south of the Kamchatka Peninsula. This brought the *Montebello* within sight of a Japanese Navy destroyer, according to Ordinary Seaman and crewmember Richard Quincy, a concern of considerable measure.[4] Japan was an ally of Germany and part of the Tripartite Pact between Germany, Italy, and Japan—a military alliance to aide each in their expansionist ambitions.

Andreasen and the *Montebello* escaped the encounter with little more than a brief trailing by the warship. But the next brush the Union Oil tanker would have with the Imperial Japanese Navy—only three months later—would produce a dramatically different outcome.

The other name connected, and far more indelibly, with the ultimate fate of the ship is Olof Ekstrom. It was Ekstrom who would replace Andreasen at the helm of the *Montebello* the night

Captain Olof Ekstrom

of her last voyage. Interestingly, he had served aboard ship with Andreasen numerous times prior to that final voyage. Olof was an experienced shipmaster, reliable and calm. But it was he who would be in command when the torpedo from the Japanese submarine was bearing down on the *Montebello*; and it was he who would face the pressure of testifying on Union Oil's behalf in the legal battle that followed.

Born in Sweden in 1895,

Ekstrom grew up in Karlskrona, a city spread over thirty islands beside the Baltic Sea. At age fourteen, he began a two-year stint working on Swedish School ships. Later, in 1915 and 1916, he served in the Swedish Navy.

At the conclusion of World War I, Ekstrom began his career on merchant ships and immigrated to the United States. He arrived in New York Harbor in 1919 aboard the *Tasmonic*—with the declared occupation of "sailor." It would be 1926 before he became a naturalized citizen. Ekstrom took his Oath of Allegiance on August 27 of that year, renouncing, as was the standard practice, "any and all allegiance to King Gustav V of Sweden."

From New York, he decided to come west, quickly finding work with several steamship companies operating along the Pacific Coast sea lanes. Ekstrom's experience soon landed him employment with Union Oil and its fleet of oil tankers. Hired in 1926, Olof began working his way up, from quartermaster to third mate, then second mate, chief mate, and finally to Master. In addition to the *Montebello,* Ekstrom would, over the years, sail in various capacities on most of the company's Pacific vessels, including the SS *Whittier, Santa Maria, La Placentia* (*Montebello's* sister ship), *Warwick, Deroche, A.C. Rubel,* and the oddly named SS *Oleum*— derived from the last half of the word "petroleum." A review of available crew manifests indicates he served most frequently on the *La Placentia* and *Montebello.*

When not at sea, Ekstrom lived in the Los Angeles suburb of Inglewood—only twenty miles from the Port of San Pedro. By 1935, he had married Olga Schmid, the daughter of Bohemian immigrants from the Czechoslovakian region.

He'd help transport oil on voyages to Manila, Singapore, the Far East, Panama Canal Zone, Hawaii, and Cuba. Though the nature of the business took Ekstrom to nearly all corners of the Pacific, the sea lane he traveled most frequently was from Port San Luis to Vancouver, B.C.—a voyage he would later estimate to have made in excess of three-hundred times. A significant exception was the *Montebello's* September 1941 trip to the U.S.S.R., the voyage to deliver fuel in which Ekstrom served as first mate to Mogens Andreasen.

"San Simeon is a small village with a group of conspicuous white buildings. There is a general store where a few provisions can be obtained; a post office is located in the wharf shed. The wharf extends into 16 feet of water and fresh water has been piped to the head of the dock where it can be taken aboard with a long hose. There are telephone facilities in the village and daily bus service to San Luis Obispo.

"An airplane landing field is located about a half mile northeastward of the wharf and is marked by a lighted air beacon. The landing field and dwellings, with the exception of the store, are the property of William Randolph Hearst, whose prominent house, a castle-like structure, is situated about 2.75 miles east-northeastward of the village at an elevation of 1,602 feet above the water. Two turrets in the house are kept lighted at night and are visible well out to seaward."

—UNITED STATES *COAST PILOT*, 1942

Chapter Five

Between Peace and War

There were moments as he walked the trails of the light station that Norman Francis would reflect on the decade past. It had been a fortunate one for him. While the Great Depression had devastated so many Americans, he'd had steady employment throughout the 1930s.

He'd joined the United States Lighthouse Service a year before the stock market crash of 1929. The hard economic times of the Depression ruined many financial empires. But it hadn't eliminated the need for lighthouses—and the keepers who maintained them. Every mariner depended on the beacons for the safety of cargo, crew, and vessel. Aides-to-navigation, as they always did, remained essential.

Francis thought of his initial career assignment—at Point Reyes Light Station—where he'd first learned the ropes as an assistant light keeper. And how, by 1930, he had been promoted to first assistant at Point Arguello, a solitary lighthouse location north of Point Conception. Norman's career path would take him to one more stop, Los Angeles Harbor Light, before landing him in 1935 at an assignment he would come to love—Piedras Blancas Light

Piedras Blancas Light Station as it appeared in 1941.
(Piedras Blancas Light Station.org)

Station.

Francis was thirty-five years old when he arrived and recognized quickly the nineteen-acre lighthouse reservation was ideal for him and his family. The station was "in the country" and yet a mere five miles from the village of San Simeon. It was also considered a "school station." The children, Norman Jr., twelve, and Leonora Elise, eleven, could attend grammar school in Cambria—only twelve miles away. Groceries and necessary items could be purchased at Soto's Market in town, or, in a pinch, procured at little Sebastian's Store in San Simeon.

The keepers' dwelling at the station was a good match for the Francis family's needs. And the setting at Piedras Blancas proved idyllic. The point, which extended a half-mile out to sea, was surrounded on three sides by an azure blue ocean. The shoreline—majestic in all weather—was a persistent rocky bluff lined at the water by swaying brown kelp.

Immediately north of the station rose the Santa Lucia mountain range that hugged the coastline. Known as Big Sur, this steep and cragged land stretched north for 90 miles to the mouth of the

Carmel River—a coastline so rugged poet Robinson Jeffers called it, "that jagged country which nothing but a fallen meteor will ever plow."

To the station's east and south lay the vast property owned by the famed tycoon and newspaper publisher William Randolph Hearst, with its rolling hills and ranchlands. The coastal cliffs were muted here. Grasses, browned by the parched summer season, covered the lower slopes that rose gently toward the hills beyond. Clusters of oak trees spotted the hillsides like patches sewn on a quilt.

Work was arduous, and at the light station, never-ending. Francis and his assistant keepers maintained regular shifts of operation and upkeep for virtually everything at Piedras Blancas: buildings, fences, plumbing, grounds, the water tower, and the oil house.

But the primary focus was always the light: the giant first-order Fresnel lens atop the conical tower, 158 feet above sea level. When the men were "on-watch" it was the light they attended to. The light source and rotation (which produced the flash of the beacon) and the foghorn signal could not be allowed to fail—ever. Both the light and the hoarse bellow of the foghorn were timed frequently by the keepers—and adjusted as necessary—to carefully preserve their characteristic: in the light's case, two white flashes

San Simeon, 1941. (Courtesy of California Military Museum)

every fifteen seconds.

By 1939, the Lighthouse Service, in a government cost-cutting measure, had been absorbed by the United States Coast Guard. Francis was now "Officer-in-Charge," a change from the more alluring title of "Head Keeper." Aside from that, life was good for the Francis family as the calendar turned to 1941. The light station provided an appealing blend of a rugged but wonderful lifestyle.

They had interesting neighbors, too, in the township of San Simeon: ranch hands, cowboys, blacksmiths, gardeners, electricians, mechanics, dairymen, and poultrymen. What made these people unique? Virtually everyone in the village worked for William Randolph Hearst.

The enormously wealthy publisher owned twenty-eight papers at his peak, most of them large dailies, and was worth $3.1 billion, or more than $30 billion in today's dollars. He lived just up the hill from the village—at what is now known as Hearst Castle but what WRH then called, "the ranch." Few coastal townships had residents with such occupations as horticulturist, zoologist, animal attendant, projectionist, marble worker, butler, and chauffer. Yet, that was the citizenry of San Simeon in 1941.

That year, Norman Francis received a salary of $1,500—the average annual income in America was $2,050. But family housing was provided by the government at the light station, thus saving the thirty-dollar monthly rent he would have paid for a home in Cambria. When his wife, Florence, needed dairy products, she could find milk at Soto's for twenty-seven cents a half-gallon and award-winning butter from the Harmony Valley Creamery for forty-one cents a pound. The Chevron Station on Main Street charged nineteen cents for a gallon of gasoline. And a ticket at the Cambria Theater would cost the moviegoer thirty-nine cents.

In 1941, the movie *Citizen Kane*—based in part on a thinly veiled model of Hearst—would fail to win the Oscar for Best Picture as expected. Hearst, who resented the self-absorbed and power-hungry portrayal of himself, refused to allow mention of the film in any Hearst newspaper. To his pleasure, *How Green Was*

My Valley won the Oscar.

At the light station two other families lived along-side the Francis's. Assistant keepers Ray Davis and Clifford McBeth's households each had two children. All were younger than the Francis teenagers who, by then, were seventeen and sixteen years of age.

Also on the station was a longtime assistant keeper, Joseph Harrington. He had been born in Ireland in 1874 and joined the Lighthouse Service in 1911. Harrington and his wife, Marion, had first been assigned to the isolated Punta Gorda Lighthouse near Cape Mendocino. In 1926, the Harrington's were transferred to Piedras Blancas. He served at the light station nine years prior to Norman Francis's arrival, and then alongside him for five more. Now sixty-six, the reliable Irishman, widowed only a few years earlier, stood every watch and duty assigned him and was a man Francis knew he could count on.

Financial indicators had improved significantly by 1941, returning to pre-Depression levels. The upbeat mood, however, that accompanied the better economic times among the residents of the small towns along the Central Coast—and across America—was tempered by world events. Optimism and reality were in conflict.

Europe was at war.

In September 1939, peace had been shattered by Nazi Germany's invasion of Poland. The following April, Germany overran Belgium, the Netherlands, and Luxembourg. In May 1940, German forces swept across France and, by months end, had bottled up the British Expeditionary Force in a small town—only ten kilometers from the Belgian border—called Dunkirk.

The war in Europe expanded still further in April 1941 when Germany marched into Yugoslavia and Greece, followed by the massive Nazi invasion of the Soviet Union on June 22.

Meanwhile, there existed an isolationist sentiment among many in the United States; a belief that America should do all it could to stay out of the war. Others were convinced the U.S.

**Soldiers from Camp San Luis Obispo at Sebastian's Store, San Simeon, 1941.
(Courtesy of the California Military Museum)**

would eventually be drawn into the war and preparation for such a scenario was necessary. President Roosevelt had pushed forward the Selective Training and Service Act of 1940—the first peacetime draft—and signed into law the Lend-Lease Act in March 1941, allowing America to ship war supplies to the Allies in Europe.

Talk of war had become commonplace in Washington, D.C. Across the nation, the looming specter of hostilities was like an approaching storm. There was little, it seemed, that could be done to avoid it.

In the Far East, the Empire of Japan had been engaged for ten years in military expansion. Japanese troops had mercilessly invaded areas of China and Southeast Asia, which the country's forces now occupied. In response, Roosevelt had ordered the seizure of all Japanese assets in the United States and imposed an oil embargo in an attempt to pressure Japan to withdraw from the occupied territories.

Army camps across the United States were being refurbished—or new ones constructed—during this time of mobilization sparked by the potential for war. Locally, Camp San Luis Obispo—located roughly halfway between SLO and Morro Bay—had been established in 1928. By 1940 the Army began training there and the camp became home to the 40th Infantry Division. Training sites included artillery, small arms, mortar, and grenade ranges.

Eighteen thousand soldiers were stationed at Camp SLO, preparing for deployment to the Pacific and European theaters should war break out. Hundreds more were stationed at the Morro Bay Amphibious Training Base. Instruction for operating Navy patrol vessels and landing craft took place on the base at the north edge of the town.

With the threat of war, the demand for oil distribution only increased. Canada, aiding the British Commonwealth's war effort, was desperately short on fuel, the province of British Columbia in particular. The Union Oil tanker SS *Montebello* made frequent—and much needed—voyages to deliver crude to facilities in Vancouver, B.C.

On December 5, two days before the attack on Pearl Harbor, the *Montebello*, having unloaded its cargo, shipped out of

115th Regiment amphibious exercises at Morro Bay, 1941. The Amphibious Base
was located at the current site of the Duke Energy Power Plant.
(California Military Museum)

The SS *Montebello* was 440 feet in length. The vessel displaced 8,272 tons.

Vancouver bound for Port San Luis, and was expected to arrive three days later. Mogens Andreasen, assisted by first mate Olof Ekstrom and a crew of thirty-six seamen, captained the vessel. The ship had just marked twenty years of service, its record of service pristine, its owners, officers and crew justifiably proud.

The weather was fair on December 6, 1941, at Piedras Blancas Light Station. There had been light fog that morning but it soon dissipated, replaced by blue skies and a capricious Pacific breeze. Temperatures would reach a high of sixty-five degrees. It was a Saturday, and families on the lighthouse reservation were listening to the radio—as all Americans did: comedies, music, and news.

That evening, radio broadcasts announced Franklin Roosevelt had addressed a personal message to Emperor Hirohito asking Japan's cooperation in the maintenance of peace in the Pacific. "The announcement of Roosevelt's dramatic appeal," wrote the *Salinas Morning Post*, "was believed to be the first time a president has ever sent a personal note to the Emperor of Japan." Meanwhile, the Japanese press noted, "negotiations [with the United States] might fail completely at any moment."

At the same time Roosevelt's radio message went forth on that December evening, the Imperial Japanese Navy submarine

I-21, commanded by Kanji Matsumura, was on patrol 120 miles north of Hawaii, providing security for the fleet naval strike force. Meanwhile, six aircraft carriers were making final preparations for the next day's surprise attack; 354 dive-bombers, fighters, and torpedo planes were now fueled and armed for the assault on the United States Pacific Fleet anchored at Pearl Harbor.

Chapter Six

Explosions

December 22, 1941, began as an ordinary Monday for Arline Genardini in the quiet coastal village of Cayucos. The high temperature would reach fifty-eight degrees and the wind, as was its habit, swept in from the Pacific Ocean to add a chill to the winter air. The sparse traffic along California's State Highway 1 rolled through the middle of town—and past the Cayucos Garage, an auto-repair shop owned and managed by Arline's husband Roy.

The Genardinis lived on C Street—just a short distance from the ocean and directly up the road from the wharf. Roy's garage was his full-time employment, but for many years he also carried the title of town constable. When trouble arose in one form or another, Roy, who residents described as "a mountain of a man," would wipe his hands, change into his uniform, and deal with it. In 1941, trouble on the Central Coast was rare. But that was about to change.

In the evening, the temperature dropped to forty-four degrees. A light drizzle began to fall. As he and Arline turned out the lights that night and retired to bed, they could have little imagined the events that would jolt them from their sleep. It happened at 3 AM.

Explosions heard on December 23, 1941 awakened everyone
in the quiet coastal village of Cayucos.

Ka-boom!
An explosion at sea.
Ka-boom!
A second.

Then came a third, a thunderous boom so severe Arline would
later say, "It nearly threw me out of bed." Houses in Cayucos and
Morro Bay were shaken to their foundation. Even residents in San
Luis Obispo—thirteen miles inland—reported windows rattling.

The bay was obscured by the rain and mist, making it impossible
for Arline or Roy to determine just what had happened. But a
short distance away, C. Ross Spooner, a rancher on the tip of
Point Estero—just north of Cayucos—had a better view through
a break in the weather. He hurriedly telephoned the sheriff's office
to report seeing "three flashes of light" offshore. Along with those,
he had heard three minor blasts in the dark—followed by one
immense flash and a booming explosion.

Twenty-eight miles to the north, Norman Francis was preparing to begin his duty shift at Piedras Blancas Light Station. The officer-in-charge was scheduled to be on-watch from 4 AM to 8 AM.
Shortly after the explosions off Cayucos, he received a report from
the Army base at Estero; a submarine was prowling off the bay.
Francis woke his crew, grabbed his assistant Joseph Harrington,

and set six men in positions around and atop the light tower to watch for any enemy action.

What the Genardinis and virtually every resident along the coast had heard in those pre-dawn hours was the *I-21*'s attack of the 430-foot Richfield oil tanker SS *Larry*

Norman Francis (L) with son Norman Jr. during the war.

Doheny. Approximately three or four miles off Morro Rock, the *I-21* had fired two salvos from her deck gun. In the darkness and pitching seas, the shells had missed their target. The *Larry Doheny*'s veteran captain, Norwegian-born O.S. Breiland, ordered the ship into a series of zigzag maneuvers.

Several minutes later, the *I-21* fired one torpedo.[5] The tremendous flash and concussion seen by Spooner at his ranch—and felt by the Genardinis in bed—was the Type-95 torpedo that had missed the *Larry Doheny* and detonated, either by hitting floating debris or, more likely, being triggered by the wake of the ship. Visibility was poor. Matsumura may well have believed

The SS *Larry Doheny* fully-laiden and riding low in the water.

the torpedo struck its target and decided to break off the attack and submerge. The *Larry Doheny* raced for the shallow waters of Estero Bay just north of Morro Rock, seeking shelter. It docked at the Standard Oil Pier there.

It wasn't the ship's first escape from disaster. Seven years earlier, the tanker had been pounded by a South Pacific typhoon—in Force Ten conditions—with the violence of gigantic battering rams. Thought to have been lost when her frantic distress calls were suddenly silenced by storm damage to the ship's radio equipment, the tanker somehow survived and limped to the haven at the Island of Guam for inspections and repairs. Now, on this dark December morning in 1941, luck had again been on the *Larry Doheny's* side.

"When daylight came," wrote the *Santa Cruz Evening News*, "Mrs. Genardini said she saw a tanker tied up at the oil loading station at Estero Bay. She expressed the opinion that the boat may have been chased into the bay as the result of the fight. She was unable to identify the tanker with her field glasses."

Arline proved to be an accurate observer. At the same time the constable's wife had been peering through her binoculars, rumors of another attack began spreading through town. A ship had been torpedoed, people said, south of the lighthouse near San Simeon. Constable Genardini drove north on the coast road to the seaside town of Cambria to investigate. When he arrived, he discovered the rumors were true.

A ship *had* been torpedoed. Townspeople who gathered at the beaches claimed to have seen in the distance what appeared to be a ship's stern rise from the water and disappear. And at the light station, Norman Francis and his men had observed gun flashes at sea around 5:45 A.M. By noon, the vessel had been officially identified. It was Union Oil's SS *Montebello.*

Chapter Seven

Stalked

By 1941, a constant procession of ocean traffic flowed up and down the West Coast of North America, from Vancouver, B.C., to San Diego, California—and beyond. But the peaceful passage of shipping along those sea lanes had come to a shocking and abrupt halt only eleven days after the Japanese attack at Pearl Harbor.

Japan had shown that the long reach of the Empire's military capability was far greater than anyone had previously thought, striking not only the territory of Hawaii but also the coastal waters of the continental United States more than 5,000 miles away.

In the days following December 7, the nine Japanese submarines assigned to sail east from Hawaiian waters had arrived at strategic positions along the West Coast of North America. The designated locations for each submarine to initiate their patrols included:

I-10 off San Diego
I-19 off Los Angeles Harbor
I-21 off Point Arguello/Estero Bay

I-23 off Monterey Bay
I-15 off Golden Gate Bridge, San Francisco
I-17 off Cape Mendocino
I-9 off Cape Blanco, Oregon
I-25 off the mouth of the Columbia River, Oregon
I-26 off the Strait of San Juan de Fuca, Washington

The December 22, 1941, *Des Moines Register* reported Japan had 40 submarines capable of operating off the U.S. West Coast.

The hunting of merchant shipping began promptly and attacks came in rapid succession. At least four ships had been attacked in the seventy-two hours prior to the *Montebello* sailing from Port San Luis that December 23.

One hour before dawn on December 18, off Cape Mendocino, the first blow was struck. The freighter *Samoa* was on her normal route between Astoria, Oregon, and San Diego. She had encountered the submarine *I-17,* commanded by Kozo Nishino. Five projectiles were fired from the deck gun of the *I-17* followed by the launch of one torpedo. The *Samoa* escaped any serious damage when the torpedo passed directly underneath the shallow-draft vessel without touching the hull and exploded a short distance away in a huge shower of water, smoke, and flame. Visibility was very poor that morning and Nishino, believing he had struck his target, submerged and withdrew. The *Samoa* safely reached San Diego.

Two days later, December 20, the Richfield Oil Company's *SS Agwiworld* was north-bound twenty miles off Cypress Point. About five-hundred yards to her port side, the *I-23* shelled the tanker with her deck gun.

The ship's captain began zigzag maneuvers and laid a heavy smoke screen as she entered Monterey Bay and raced for Santa Cruz. In the heavily pitching sea both the accuracy and safety of the *I-23's* gun crew were compromised. The submarine's captain broke off the pursuit.

The *Agwiworld* escaped and docked beside the pier at Santa Cruz without damage. That evening, an article appearing in the *Monterey Peninsula Herald* said, "Scores of golfers playing seaside courses reported today they had observed the tanker with huge clouds of smoke pouring from her funnel, fleeing toward Santa Cruz and zigzagging wildly, but most of them thought little more about it."

That same afternoon, December 20, eight miles west of Cape Mendocino, the SS *Emidio* would be less fortunate. The General Petroleum tanker was two-hundred miles north of San Francisco sailing in ballast from Seattle to Ventura when she was discovered by the *I-17*.

The submarine's deck gun began firing salvos. The *Emidio's* captain sent an S.O.S. through the radio operator, followed by the message, "Under attack by enemy sub." Then he hoisted a white flag and ordered his men to the lifeboats.

Attempting to launch one of the boats, three sailors were killed when a shell struck the lifeboat and detonated. The men were blasted into the water and never found.

Minutes later, the submarine drove a torpedo into the stern-section of the hull, killing two more of the crew. The 435-foot tanker, though badly crippled, didn't sink. She drifted for several days, a total of eighty-five miles, before running aground

First Pacific Coast Torpedoed Ship. "General Petroleum Tanker Emidio," torpedoed by Japanese Dec. 19, 1941 off Eureka Coast, as it appeared after floating to Crescent City, Calif, on Dec. 20, 1941.

The SS *Emido* aground on rocks at Crescent City, California.

on rocks near Crescent City. She was never re-floated. The U.S. Coast Guard vessel *Shawnee* picked up thirty-one survivors; five men died in the attack.

Several days later, and well down the coast at Point Arguello, fourteen-year-old Jack Sudden, son of a ranch superintendent, was rabbit hunting along the Southern Pacific Railroad tracks. It was 8:30 AM when the ninth grader's attention was drawn to the sound of an explosion offshore.

Only two miles away, Jack could plainly see the Standard Oil Company tanker *H.M. Storey* being chased by a submarine running on the surface. The sub fired several salvos from the deck gun as the *H.M. Storey* attempted to use a thick smoke screen for protection.

The ship's master later told the *Lompoc Recorder*, "One torpedo was fired [at us] in addition to shells from the deck." Fortunately for the ship, the shells and torpedo all missed their target. The *I-19* submerged and fled the area.

Witnesses said Army patrol planes had responded quickly to the tanker's radio call, promptly circled over the fight scene, and dropped several depth bombs. "The shoreline from Conception to Surf," the newspaper said, "was shaken by the explosion of the depth bombs."

Chapter Eight

A Foreboding Departure

Mogens Andreasen and the *Montebello* crew had just completed a delivery to the facilities at Vancouver the previous week. On her southern return, the tanker passed within sight of Victoria as she coursed through the Strait of San Juan de Fuca. As Andreasen cleared Cape Flattery, he routed the tanker south, and over the next seven hundred miles sailed past the mouth of the Columbia River, beyond the Oregon-California border, past Cape Mendocino and San Francisco's Golden Gate Bridge. It would be good to reach home at Port San Luis—even more so with war having begun just two weeks before.

How much things had changed since the *Montebello* had sailed to the Soviet Union only a few months ago.

It was Sunday, December 21, 1941. The tanker surged past Point Buchon and, within an hour, swung into port and tied up at Union Oil's quay on Middle Dock. The next day was quiet in Avila. Oil workers were busy pumping more than 75,000 barrels—in excess of three million gallons—of Santa Maria crude oil into the holds of the *Montebello*.

Considered "heavy" with a gravity of 21.81, the oil had to be

SS *Montebello* in Los Angeles Harbor.

warmed prior to loading or discharge, and the *Montebello* was equipped with a cargo heating system to do just that. Also pumped aboard were 2,477 barrels of bunker fuel—used to power the vessel itself—for the ship's next passage to Vancouver.

By the following day, preparations had been made to sail. It would be a Christmas at sea for the crew. Routing and departure permits were received and authorities had cleared the *Montebello* to sail early on December 22.

But the submarine attacks on merchant ships the previous few days had created worry among the crew. A handful threatened not to sail. There was talk of war-risk insurance, a component of which included war-risk liability. Such coverage would compensate for the loss of people and personal items inside the vessel; several of the *Montebello's* crew were demanding it.

A resounding lack-of-agreement existed between Union Oil and the small number of balking sailors aboard the ship. The company's response was swift and decisive; such insurance would *not* be offered the crew—if necessary, the company vowed to bus replacements from Los Angeles to Avila for those who refused to sail.

Details of the pre-sailing dispute were recorded in a letter written on December 24 by Earnest Fay James, a forty-six-year-old deputy collector from the U.S. Customs House at Avila. In his letter addressed to the Collector of Customs in Los Angeles, James, stated:

Owing to crew trouble over the payment of war risk insurance this sailing was delayed until crew replacements could arrive up here from Los Angeles. At 8 PM, December 22, 1941, the writer was informed by Mr. Shekelle, local agent of the Union Oil Company, that those crew replacements would arrive before midnight, that later Naval routings had been received and that it was desired to sail the vessel just as soon as they could ...

A popular belief became, in later years, that the *Montebello's* entire crew had been replaced and Captain Andreasen had refused to sail. But the evidence suggests otherwise. Nearly all of the crew who had sailed with the captain on voyages to Vancouver earlier in December would again sail aboard the *Montebello* on the night of

The Union Oil pier was fitted with pipes carrying various grades of crude oil to be pumped onto the ships. These vessels are preparing to load.
(History Center of San Luis Obispo County)

the attack. Only six new names appear on the last crew manifest. In regard to Mogens Andreasen, he had been, by now, a loyal captain in the company's fleet since 1916. He had faced every threat the world's oceans had hurled at him. Rather than Andreasen refusing to sail, evidence indicates he was sick. E.F. James's notation—in the same letter—stated, "... there would also be a change of Masters, Captain M. Andreasen having become ill."

A Swedish-born sailor who had previously served as Mogens's first officer, Olof Walfrid Ekstrom, was slated to work this voyage as chief officer. But with Andreasen's illness, the company needed a new captain—and Union Oil had an excellent option available in Ekstrom. Olof was qualified to master any of the company's vessels, and, according to crewman Richard Quincy, was reputed to have good relations with his crews. The new captain was extremely familiar with the ship and her qualities, having served aboard the *Montebello* and *La Placentia* for lengthy periods of time.

Night settled in. It was dark by 5:20 PM and the lights came on along Avila's Front Street. The tanker rested at Middle Dock with her bow facing seaward. Some nights, especially in the winter when less coastal fog appeared, the skies above the Central Coast were awash with stars. But not this night. A thin crescent moon had risen above the horizon but was hardly visible through the light rain that had begun to fall. Off the port side, the few lights still burning late at night in Avila, a half-mile distant, sprinkled the darkness. To starboard stood the old Harford Wharf. The hillsides that surrounded the bay were black silhouettes—even at midnight—against the sky.

The bus from Los Angeles arrived and dropped off the Union crew replacements. Aboard the ship, the six new merchant sailors were signed to the crew manifest and the vessel's papers were corrected to reflect the changes. With that accomplished, the Deputy Customs Officer walked across the deck of the *Montebello,* down the gangplank, and left the ship. It was just past midnight—12:20 AM. The ship's boilers had been warm for hours, the 3,300-horsepower engine waiting to be engaged. From the bridge wings,

Ekstrom checked both port and starboard sides and gave orders to raise the gangplank and cast off bow and stern lines. Then, to the quartermaster at the helm, John McIsaac, the captain said, "Take her out!" The ship's four-bladed, eighteen-foot propeller gradually started to swirl and, like an inchworm, the *Montebello* slowly began to glide forward. At 1:30 AM, now Tuesday, December 23, the tanker left Middle Dock. She soon cleared Port San Luis and was abeam of the breakwater headed for open sea.

As the *Montebello* rounded the breakwater, officers on the bridge, through the dark drizzle, could barely see to starboard the red-then-white flash of the Point San Luis Obispo Lighthouse. Once beyond, the vessel began increasing speed, the humming of her engine now more pronounced. Soon, she was churning north at ten knots. The ship was outbound to the Union Oil refinery in Vancouver, B.C., a voyage she had successfully made on hundreds of occasions.

The conditions, however, were different this time. The crew of the tanker knew Japanese submarines were stalking coastal shipping. They were well aware of the risk they faced. The portholes had been covered and wheelhouse lights lowered to expose as little lumination as possible.

The middle third of the bridge was occupied by the wheelhouse. There, in darkened conditions, Ekstrom, chief officer Kenneth McLean, and first mate John Young were busy laying a course northwestward. The ship's wind-snapped halyards clanged against the masts fore and aft of the wheelhouse.

It was another nine miles before the *Montebello* would clear Point Buchon. Ekstrom knew to take care here; there were numerous outlying rocks and sunken ledges that, in some cases, extended over a mile from shore. The smooth glide of the ship the crew had felt inside the breakwater was now replaced by the up-and-down lunging of open water.

Though the light rain was little more than a mist, it was still unwelcomed. The drizzle, slung by fifteen mile-per-hour headwinds, stung any skin exposed to the bitterly cold forty-two-degree air. The vessel's decks had become slippery; the ladder steps and railings were now slick.

The ship rounded Point Buchon at 2:34 AM, well beyond the lighted whistle buoy one mile off the point. From there, Ekstrom laid a new course, again northwest, to pass several miles beyond Piedras Blancas Light Station. The *Montebello* plowed forward, still at ten knots, into the undulating seas, past Morro Rock.

Then it happened: near 3 AM, multiple explosions boomed in the distance.[6] Ekstrom quickly emerged on the wing and looked astern. He saw yellow bursts of gun flashes through the darkness, followed by a reverberating boom that rolled toward him. Three miles to his stern—maybe four—Olof wasn't sure. He realized instantly, with the explosions behind him, he could not turn back for Port San Luis. His only option was to press forward.

"Make all possible speed…and disregard all safety precautions for speed!" he said on the phone to the engine room.

As the engineer increased power, the drone of the ship's engine vibrated through the vessel—the hum slightly louder now and higher in pitch.

Several miles astern of the *Montebello,* the Richfield oil tanker SS *Larry Doheny* was under attack—and in trouble. The ship had sent out a message—picked up by *Montebello's* radio operator William Barnhart: "Attacked by enemy raider three miles off Estero Bay."

In a desperate attempt to evade her assailant, the *Larry Doheny* had begun evasive maneuvers and raced toward Estero Bay in the hopes of finding safety in the shallow waters.

Meanwhile, Ekstrom kept his ship churning northwest—with great urgency—at her maximum speed of eleven knots. Perhaps, he thought, he could put distance between the tanker and submarine; maybe enough to discourage a pursuit. But the *I-21,* under Commander Matsumura, was able to climb to a surface speed of twenty-four knots and was easily capable of closing a gap of miles. The *Montebello's* captain knew he could soon be in the crosshairs of the submarine's periscope. Adrenaline pulsed through his veins and every man on the ship.

"All crew don lifejackets!" he ordered.

At 5:30 AM, the *Montebello's* already-desperate situation turned even worse. Her lookouts had spotted a submarine.[7] The *I-21* had reeled in its prey and was now lurking in the *Montebello's* wake—nearly a mile astern. Ekstrom placed chief officer McLean and able-bodied seaman William Frez at the stern of the vessel. From there, the men had better sightlines to track the sub.

Ekstrom called through the speaking tube to the radio operator to send a message, "S.O.S. Submarine trying to attack." The captain called the engine room for extra speed, then gave the order to McIsaac, at the helm, "Hard right rudder!" The oil-bloated *Montebello* slowly began to swing—the first of several zigzag maneuvers she would complete. After nearly a minute, as the ship swung right, McIsaac eased the rudder and held until the next Ekstrom order came.

"Hard left!"

For about ten minutes the *Montebello* desperately alternated right and left zigzags. Meanwhile, Quincy, McLean and Frez teamed to relay the submarine's every change of distance and position. As he quickly shifted from one wing of the bridge to the other, Ekstrom could see the silhouette of the submarine. The distance was closing. A mile. Three quarters of a mile. Nearly half a mile.

Aboard the *I-21*, Matsumura had now positioned his boat to the inland side of the tanker, looking for the optimal point from which to begin his attack. He submerged to periscope depth, knowing that would stabilize the sub for the shot.

As the tanker neared reaching a right angle, he could wait no longer. He launched a single Type-95 torpedo—and began counting the seconds. Knifing through the water at fifty miles an hour, the torpedo skipped several times above the waves, as a crewman would later recall, ducking below water again by the sheer weight of the 3,671-pound weapon.

About forty seconds after launching from the tube, the torpedo had traveled the nine-hundred yards between the *I-21* and the *Montebello*. It slammed into the starboard side of the tanker and exploded in a gigantic plume of water and smoke. The nearly half-ton warhead ripped a hole through the ship's side, causing the riveted steel-plated hull to buckle like a tin can. The missile detonated with such tremendous force that the entire 440-foot tanker lurched and swung leftward. It was 5:45 AM. All was dark.

The massive concussion knocked the entire crew to the floor. Anything that hadn't been bolted down flew to port or starboard, fore or aft. The *Montebello* began to shudder, then slowed to a stop. The officers and helmsman struggled to regain their feet. Captain Ekstrom called radioman Barnhart to send another message.

"The wireless has been knocked out," said Barnhart.

"Use the emergency radio," said Ekstrom.

But that, too, was out of commission. So was the ship's rudder. All lights were out. The captain sent a message down to the engine room, "Secure the fires and shut the boilers down."

By some miracle, the *Montebello's* volatile cargo had not immediately blown sky-high. The crude oil she carried had a low flash point—meaning the cargo was highly combustible. If the torpedo had struck one of the tanks containing oil, the fire of the blast would have ignited the cargo resulting in a catastrophic explosion.[8] Though no flames had yet ignited from the blast, the fear of fire petrified the crew; flames posed a greater threat than sinking—and the men aboard knew it. Ekstrom could still smell the oakite burning from the TNT.

The general alarm rang and confusion reigned. The electrical system failed; the beams from flashlights gyrated here and there. The captain had been thrown to the floor by the explosion and had lost his flashlight in the process. Leaving the blackened wheelhouse, he made an effort to retrieve the ship's money and property from the safe. But by the light of a match, Ekstrom could not open the dial-combination safe. Log books, deviation books, money—everything would have to be left in an effort to escape and survive. He grabbed a lifejacket as he left the room.

All hands scurried up on deck, and in the pre-dawn darkness, all were accounted for. To this point, Ekstrom could at least be thankful there had been no loss of life or injury.

"The ship won't sink right away," he told the men, "Stay calm and stand by with the [life] boats out."

But ten minutes after the torpedo strike, the men of the *Montebello* received a second scare. The *I-21* had surfaced in the distance—the boat's gunnery crew manning the submarine's deck gun—and began shelling the crippled tanker to speed her sinking. For the ship's crew, this only increased the odds of a shell penetrating one of the eighteen tanks containing oil and killing them all in a fireball. One salvo snapped the foremast. Another projectile exploded close to the No. 1 lifeboat near the stern. Six or seven shells had been fired from the sub's deck gun, Ekstrom would later estimate.

The ship was dead in the water, which proved helpful now. The absence of any forward momentum made it possible to launch the lifeboats. Still, with the boats mounted on davits near the stern and the ship settling bow first, there was little time to lose. The boats needed to be lowered fast—before they rose too far above the sea to safely launch.

Thirty-two men scrambled into three lifeboats on the opposite side of the ship away from the shelling. It was now nearly 6:10 AM, and though still dark, the horizon was discernible. The crew could see the black outline of the hills above San Simeon and Cambria.

Two boats were lowered off the davits into the water without trouble. But the third boat was in jeopardy. The painters—lines that lower the lifeboat—were stuck. Unless they could be released, the *Montebello* would drag the boat to the bottom as she sank.

Daniel Seed, the ship's assistant engineer, was still on deck looking for a lifeboat when he heard swearing over the ship's railing. As he looked below, he realized it was coming from the trapped lifeboat. Amidst the bursts of profanity, someone found the boat axe, and in a moment of focused desperation, chopped the painters apart. Seed slid down one of the falls and into the boat; within

Photo reveals the rippled and torn lower portion of a Liberty ship named the *Peter H. Burnett*—and the tremendous explosive power of the Japanese Type-95 torpedo. The ship had been attacked by the *I-21*, the same submarine to sink the *Montebello*. The *Peter H. Burnett* survived the attack—viewed here being repaired at the Cockatoo Island Dockyards in Sydney, Australia.
(Australian War Memorial)

twenty minutes, all three were away and had rowed a safe distance from the *Montebello*.

The captain and five others had stayed with the ship—unsure if she would sink. But the bow continued to settle further below the water's surface. As the sea climbed up the deck and the ship's funnel leaned further forward, Ekstrom accepted the inevitable. The tanker would remain afloat only a short time longer.

Ekstrom, McLean, and Young entered No. 1 lifeboat along with fireman Edgar Smith, seaman Bill Frez, and John Smith, a five-foot one-inch bosun's mate who hailed from Australia.

As No. 1 was lowered to the water, the men made the worrisome discovery that the boat was slippery with oil. Worse, they found water. The lifeboat had sustained shrapnel damage from the 5-inch shell that had exploded close by. Water poured sporadically through holes near the bow. But Ekstrom and his men would have to live or die with No. 1 boat.

They were out of options.

Chapter Nine

Rescue

The *Montebello's* lifeboats bobbed up and down in the swells. The men had rowed a distance from the ship and watched helplessly as the ship settled forward and began her groaning death throes. In the drizzle and dim light of dawn, the crew watched as the bow submerged completely and the stern of the ship slowly began to elevate. Seeing the rear third of the vessel rising above the water brought home the sheer size of the ship the men had sailed upon so often.

The propeller and rudder ascended higher until the end of the tanker stood vertically 150 feet above the water "like a telephone pole," several witnesses would later say. Then, at 6:45 AM, an hour after the torpedo had shattered her hull, the *Montebello* began to plunge straight down as the propeller, rudder, railing, and flagstaff disappeared in succession beneath the ocean surface.

The *I-21* didn't linger to witness the *Montebello's* final moments. Confident in the mortal damage his submarine had inflicted, Matsumura ordered the boat to withdraw. It quietly slid below the choppy seas—before the threat of any air patrol could arrive—and disappeared.

Meanwhile, the *Montebello's* crew shifted its survival efforts from the attack by the Imperial Japanese Navy to the precarious task of rowing miles to shore in the cold, wind, and rough seas. Conditions were harsh. The men were already shivering. Their clothing was drenched and the wind-chill off the frigid ocean water only magnified their numbness and fatigue.

The lifeboats had trouble remaining in visual contact with each other amid the surging waters and still-faint light of dawn. The ship's third mate, as the highest-ranking officer, took charge of one. Tempers flared, Richard Quincy remembered, when the boat wandered aimlessly.

"Can't you steer straight?" the officer yelled to the crewman at the rudder.

"The damn pintle is broken!" the crewman barked back. The pintle—the hinging mechanism on outboard-mounted rudders—had rusted and broken with the rudder's first movement, rendering the tiller useless.

Powered only by oars, the lifeboats were largely at the mercy of the ocean current as each crew struggled to row in the direction of what now seemed a very distant shore. The men fought to prevent the boats from capsizing in the wind-swept waves, muscling every oar stroke and steering of the rudder with frozen limbs and hands. Their thoughts were brief and simple: Stay afloat. Fight the current. Head toward shore. And watch for rescuers.

Unknown to the lifeboats, Standard Oil Company tugboats the *Alma*, captained by Merle Molinari, and the *Estero*, by Pete Stocking, were lying off Cayucos, waiting for an incoming tanker to arrive at the oil-loading terminal at Estero Bay. But when word reached the little Standard Oil office across the highway from the oil pier, both boats were immediately dispatched—bearing northwest—toward Piedras Blancas in search of survivors.

Near 9 AM, the *Alma* and *Estero* arrived. By then, the three *Montebello* lifeboats had pitched about in the ocean swells for more than two bone-chilling hours. The *Alma* picked up twenty-two

The *Alma* returning with survivors. (Vic Hansen)

men and the *Estero* another ten. With all the survivors aboard and lifeboats tied to the *Estero*, the tugs began the twelve-mile return to Cayucos.

After rounding Mouse Rock, just eight hundred yards off the village of Cayucos, the tugs turned in a horseshoe fashion toward the landing. The *Coast Pilot* described the wharf then as being in "a dilapidated condition." Still, few sights could have been more beautiful to the rescued seamen as the *Alma* nudged close and her lines were secured to the dock cleats. Army authorities cleared the wharf and barred all civilians from entering the area.

The crew, although shivering cold and exhausted, were otherwise uninjured. They stepped off the *Alma* and the *Estero*, wrapped themselves in blankets offered to them, and cupped their hands around tins of hot coffee.

Meanwhile, No. 1 lifeboat, unseen by Molinari and Stocking as the pilots scanned the ocean surface, was slowly progressing toward shore. The boat carried Ekstrom, McLean, Young, and Frez, plus Edgar and John Smith. They were experiencing more than their share of trouble. With their boat leaking heavily, Ekstrom had chosen to row as direct a line as possible toward the village of Cambria.

The men of No. 1 had been the last to leave the ship and were struggling to keep their wounded boat afloat. The shrapnel damage at the boat's prow caused seawater to flush into the lifeboat in spurts. The sailors had fought hours in a determined effort to reach land with four men rowing, one bailing water, and Ekstrom, standing at the stern, guiding with a boat oar. No. 1 lifeboat had apparently been a victim, too, of a faulty boat rudder.

The sound of deck gunfire and the torpedo explosion—it had blasted a massive hole in the starboard side of the *Montebello*—had drawn a crowd to the beaches of Cambria. Some witnesses reported seeing the flashes. Elizabeth Waite, a thirty-seven-year-old mother of two boys, had spotted something resembling a long pole rising from the water.

While the fate of the other survivors was unknown to the observers on shore, the plight of Ekstrom's lifeboat was becoming alarmingly obvious. The boat was being current-swept several miles south of Cambria toward a remote and rocky stretch of coastline called Sibley Ranch.[9]

Here, the shore was fringed with kelp and lined with rocky outcroppings and low cliffs. The men could see the rocks, the twenty-five-foot cliffs, and the sloping grasslands that, within a half-mile, gave way to hills covered with Monterey pines and coastal live oaks. However, Ekstrom quickly recognized a new worry—the lack of any sand beach to safely come ashore.

No. 1 was now two hundred yards out and battling the breaking waves; the lifeboat pitched precariously closer to the rocks, close to the prominent outcropping called White Rock. A group of locals—ranchers, policemen, firemen, and Cambrian residents—was anxious to provide aide. The rescuers had driven through what was then a wooded section of coastline south of Cambria called simply, "The Pines," following dirt roads onto Sibley Ranch, and gathered above the rocks.

Austin Waltz, a thirty-one-year-old newspaper printer for *The Cambrian*, had heard the attack unfold from outside his home along Coast Highway near San Simeon. Waltz hopped in his car and drove with his father Marcus, publisher of the newspaper, toward town as they tracked the lifeboat's course. Austin and Marcus were among the would-be rescuers at Sibley Ranch who stood on the rocks, throwing lifelines to the men in No. 1.

"A large swell lifted the boat in closer and most of the fellows made a jump for it," Austin said in a United Press article. But the men in the water were unable to secure a hold on the rocks and each was swept back into the sea. The waters boiling around the rocks, Austin said, seemed "full of hands and arms and heads. They were all in the water clinging to the rope or rock or trying to get a hold. We climbed down and got ropes around the men bobbing in the water, and hauled them up."

Seaman Bill Frez later identified Waltz and Jack Freebody, Cambria's fire chief, as the men who dragged him from the surf. Others teamed together at the water's edge to pull each man to safety.

Meanwhile, Ekstrom's situation had become one of life-and-death. Half-frozen and completely exhausted, the captain had nothing left. He was unable to fight for the lines thrown toward him or resist the swells sweeping him toward, and away from, the rocks. Only his life-vest kept him afloat in the roiling surf. David Chase, twenty-six, from Morro Bay, dove into the water and swam

No. 1 lifeboat reaching Sibley Ranch. Captain Olof Ekstrom can be seen in the circle, middle right. This photo of the rescue appeared in *The Cambrian.*

to reach the captain. He somehow managed to secure a line to him. The men on shore pulled both Ekstrom and the heroic Chase to safety.

Fourteen-year-old Frank Goodall had scurried down to the ranch with his older brother and witnessed the lifeboat's crash upon the rocks. Seconds from impact, Goodall watched everyone hop over the side and into the water. One remaining sailor, Edgar Smith, chose to stay in the lifeboat. In the boiling cauldron of surf, a large swell promptly lifted the bow of the boat up upon the rocks, whereupon Smith calmly climbed out without incident. Amid the scramble of rescuers anxious to provide support for the survivors safely ashore, Frank scrambled down the rocks, reached into the boat, grabbed one of the oars, and dragged it home. The waves claimed the lifeboat soon after.

Newspaper accounts said of the six rescued crewmen, "They were so cold and numb they were barely able to speak." Neil Moses, a reporter for *The Cambrian* and editor of the *Morro Bay Sun,* wrote, "The little fellow was a pitiful sight, spotted with oil, gaunt, blue, and pallid white. Some minutes later when he was lying on the ground rolled in blankets, I asked him his name. He tried hard to tell me but I couldn't make it out, his teeth chattering so." The "little fellow" Moses described was the diminutive Australian, John Smith.

"The irony of it all came when I was driving back to the printing office," Moses wrote. "Two young Japanese-American soldiers were driving the Army ambulances going up to pick up the survivors."

Ekstrom and his remaining crew were given first-aid, mostly in the form of hot coffee and blankets, and then shuttled to Cambria Pines Lodge to get warm. They remained at the lodge for only a short time. Authorities had hurriedly arranged for the men—and the others landed by tugboats at Cayucos—to be driven to the U.S. Army Hospital at Camp San Luis Obispo, eight miles inland from Morro Bay.

E.F. James, the U.S. Customs House representative, interviewed Olof Ekstrom later that evening. Ironically, James had spoken to the captain earlier that same day, near midnight, aboard the ship docked in Port San Luis. He summarized Ekstrom's comments in an initial report to the Bureau of Marine Inspection and

The hospital at Camp San Luis Obispo, circa 1940.
(California Military Museum)

Navigation in San Pedro. The following day, James would write a more detailed account of the events to the Collector of Customs in Los Angeles:

> Port San Luis, Calif.,
> December 24, 1941
>
> Collector of Customs
> Los Angeles, California
>
> Sir:
>
> Please find here enclosed a copy of a report to the Local Inspectors, Bureau of Marine Inspection and Navigation, San Pedro, California, in regard to the torpedoing and sinking yesterday of the American steam tanker *Montebello,* a short distance up the coast from this port.
>
> The *Montebello* originally was to sail from this port some time after midnight on the 21st, as routings and departure permit had been received and the vessel cleared for Vancouver, B.C. shortly before midnight of that day. Owing to crew trouble over the payment of war risk insurance, this sailing was delayed until crew replacements could arrive up here from Los Angeles.
>
> At 8 PM, December 22, 1941, the writer was informed by Mr. Shekelle, local Agent of the Union Oil Company, that these crew replacements would arrive before midnight, that later Naval routings had been received and that it was desired to sail the vessel just as soon as they could, also that there would also be a change of Masters, Captain M. Andreasen having became ill.
>
> After finishing with the crew and signing Captain Olof W. Eckstrom (*sic*) to replace Captain M. Andreasen, correcting the vessel papers etc., the writer left the vessel at 12:20 AM December 23, 1941. It has since been learned that they sailed from Port San Luis at 2:00 AM that morning.
>
> At 3:57 AM December 23, an explosion was heard that was strong enough to shake houses in San Luis Obispo, at least twenty miles away, and knowing that there were at least three tankers in this immediate locality, all fully loaded, endeavor was made to learn if they had been attacked.
>
> Shortly after daylight Custom Guards Gonyer and Hawthorne reported that the tanker *Larry Doheny* had put in at Morro Bay to

escape shelling by a submarine, a torpedo having been fired at it but having missed and exploded, also that they had been shelled by deck rifle but without effect and that no damage had been done to the vessel. Continuous rifle fire could be both heard and seen from the beach all along Morro Bay for a distance of over ten miles which seemed to be about fifteen miles at sea.

It was then learned that another tanker had been torpedoed and was sinking. This proved to be the *Montebello,* but it was not until many hours later that these survivors were brought ashore at Cayucos, California. Those landing at San Simeon were rushed to a private hospital by officers of the California State Highway Patrol who apparently disregarded the army order to take them to the Army Hospital at Camp San Luis Obispo. Later in the day they were removed to the army hospital by army ambulances.

…Last night, after he had become rested at the hospital, Captain Olof W. Eckstrom was interviewed by the writer and made the following statements.

The *Montebello* was attacked by a submarine about five minutes after it had been sighted, at 5:45 AM, by it firing a torpedo which struck on the forward starboard side at number 2 and 3 tanks; They had tried to escape by zig-zagging their course but to no effect, and in the following explosion the bridge, radio house and upper works together with the forward mast were blown away and the vessel started to sink bow first, remaining afloat only about an hour after the explosion.

In rowing away from the sinking vessel the lifeboats were shelled by the submarine with what was thought to be a 5-inch deck gun; No person was injured but one boat was hit and badly wrecked.

After being conveyed to the San Luis Sanatorium [sic] by officers of the California State Highway Patrol, Captain Ekstrom states he was subject to questioning by news reporters which continued until he was removed by the army ambulance to the hospital at Camp San Luis Obispo, later in the day.

He also states that all of the vessel papers, documents, and everything else was lost with the ship as they had no time to even get personal effects, and that the report of casualty will be filed at the home port of Los Angeles by the Union Oil Company.

At the time of the torpedoing the *Montebello* was operating under Temporary Register No. 8-F, issued at Port San Luis, California, on December 5, 1941.

For your information, it is understood that the army are at this time making an investigation to learn why Captain Ekstrom was not taken to the camp hospital in the first place, along with the other members of his crew.

Respectfully,

E.F. James,
Deputy Collector in Charge

The *Montebello* crew at Camp San Luis Obispo Hospital.

Chapter Ten

'They'll Have to Come Through Us'

It was a good day for storytelling on the Central Coast. And the locals had a great one. Between the calamities that befell the *Montebello* and, to a much lesser extent, the *Larry Doheny*, townspeople talked of little else. And with good reason. Citizens had lived through a monumental event—at least for their region—and, in some cases, actually witnessed the attacks or assisted in saving the survivors.

Stories traveled up and down the narrow two-lane highway between Morro Bay and San Simeon with amazing speed, the talebearer accounts often varying in accuracy and intrigue. The basic facts were clear enough: two ships had been attacked by a Japanese submarine and one of them sunk. But resisting the temptation to add exciting details—based on rumor or hearsay—proved a challenging task for many. There were, some said, men and oil floating off Cambria. Others told friends that American planes had depth-bombed the submarine—almost certainly sinking it.

The rumors were contagious. Word spread that shelling had

The December 23 edition of the *San Pedro News-Pilot* broke the news.

continued non-stop for hours, Japanese destroyers had been seen off the coast, and an invasion force was likely just beyond the horizon.

Of course, none of it was true.

Some newspaper accounts were major contributors to the excitement. True or not, the statements made good copy. The United Press reports—and any inaccuracy contained therein— were repeated, with small variations, in countless papers: the *Los Angeles Times, Salt Lake Telegram, Miami Herald, Shreveport Journal, Baltimore Sun,* and hundreds of others in cities, large and small, across America.

Often it was little things—such as spelling the *Montebello* captain's name as "Olaf Eckstrom" instead of the correct Olof Ekstrom, or reporting that two torpedoes had been fired at the tanker and the first was a dud. On other occasions, quotes were attributed to crewmen of the *Montebello* that simply conflicted with the facts. As when Ekstrom was quoted as saying his ship—though torpedoed—was "still able to make headway until it was attacked again two hours later." Or when Bill Frez was quoted as saying, "The fellows in the other boats were subjected to machine-gun fire…we don't know if they made it." It is almost certain Frez never said this.[10]

One of the reports that proved true was especially well received in Southern California. Olga Ekstrom, wife of Olof, had been informed the *Montebello* was torpedoed and sunk. She had, as of yet, received no word on the status of her husband. Understandably frantic in the wake of the sinking, she waited for word in their home filled with mementoes from her husband's travels—Chinese furniture and idols, a polar bear rug, chests and miniatures.

When news finally arrived at their house on Third Avenue in Inglewood, it could not have been better. Olof and his entire crew had been rescued, all reported safe, and were now recuperating at Camp San Luis Obispo Hospital after their brush with death.

Meanwhile, in Cambria, there grew a tidal wave of civic pride. The townspeople had, in fact, acquitted themselves exceptionally well. The congratulatory front-page headline that week in the town's newspaper read, "CAMBRIA RESCUES VICTIMS OF SUB." And they had.

"Our local heroes may never make the Hall of Fame," one article began, "but they are no less real heroes for that. Many eyewitnesses of the rescue, as well as the survivors themselves, have nothing but the highest praise for the heroic work of the men who risked their lives to help bring six survivors of the *Montebello* out of the rocks and breakers on Tuesday morning at Cambria Pines."

If the town had been wearing a proverbial button-down sweater, the fasteners would have popped off in rapid succession. Citizens, upon witnessing the attack, began searching for lifeboats, "and when one was spotted"—*The Cambrian* reported—"they sprung into action."

"For a community totally unused to disaster, all forces cooperated surprisingly well, in this, our first experience with war in our front yard." Witnesses notified the town's fire chief, Jack Freebody, and "all hurried down to the beach southwest of Cambria Pines Lodge."

The town's Disaster Relief Committee, so recently formed that there had been no time to coordinate details of any response plan, "turned out in force with cars and necessary supplies and handled the situation with remarkable efficiency."

Helping with the rescue work were a host of Cambrians—named at length in the paper: Ray Shamel, Bob Marshall, Dave Woodward, Joaquin Soto, Lyle Mitchell, Ralph Goodall, and Neil Moses, among others.

"Mrs. Woodward and Mrs. Howard served hot coffee to the survivors as soon as they were brought to land." The local telephone operators, the paper noted, deserved credit as well. "The way calls were handled by the operators, swamped with calls from all directions, is worthy of the highest praise."

"They didn't catch us unprepared this time, and they won't again," said Mrs. Shamel.

Indeed, Cambrians had every reason to be pleased with both their rescue response and the outcome. Not only were all the men in No. 1 lifeboat saved without serious injury—excepting some scrapes and bruises—but the feat was accomplished at considerable risk. Men who scampered down the cliffside to reach the sailors were drenched several times by large waves washing over the rocks. Freebody was scratched up when he slipped in an effort to reach one of the men being tossed about in the water. Jack had to be dragged from the sea himself. Further bravery, of course, came in the form of David Chase and his decision to dive into the surging waves to save the life of a floundering Olof Ekstrom.

In the successful lifesaving afterglow, high spirits and good humor enlivened the town. In the week to come, Fire Chief Freebody's brother in the East wrote, asking about Jack. Like many Easterners, he seemed concerned about the safety of everyone living along the coast. Jack replied that he needn't worry, "The Japanese will have to get past Cambria before they will invade New York."

Chapter Eleven

'Brother, Can You Spare a Million-Six?'

Almost immediately after the *Montebello's* sinking, Union Oil began pursuit of a claim against the federal government. They were prepared to argue that Union Oil deserved compensation for "the destruction of personal property resulting from enemy action" under the Reconstruction Finance Corporation Act.

Jerry Powell, a graduate of University of Michigan Law School, was general counsel for the company. On January 8, 1942, the attorney wrote a letter to Mr. Fayette B. Dow in Washington D.C., proposing a claim be made to the Reconstruction Finance Corporation to seek compensation for the loss of the tanker.[11]

Powell's letter provided Dow with itemized facts regarding the ship, the cargo, and their estimated value. One week later, Fayette Dow wrote to Jesse H. Jones, head of the RFC, declaring the intent of claim by Union Oil.[12]

The RFC had, in 1941, created an entity called the War Damage Corporation to provide American citizens with insurance against the risk of property damage during war when caused by action of the enemy or by U.S. defense efforts in resisting enemy attack.

On May 18, 1942, the president of Union Oil, Reese Taylor,

Jerry Powell, the attorney
who represented Union Oil.

received a letter from Powell informing him of intention to assert entitlement to both protection under the RFC Act and compensation for the value of the ship and cargo. Powell believed "an amendment ... providing RFC funds for the War Damage Corporation had made it possible for us to recover such compensation." Powell further urged, "action be taken towards having it determined that the place where the *Montebello* was sunk was under the dominion and control of the United States, so that we might prosecute our claim."

The company's legal staff began preparations for the complaint to be filed, including obtaining a sworn affidavit of the attack events by Olof Ekstrom, which was taken on January 28, 1943. That same day, Union Oil Vice-President A.C. Stewart would write the War Damage Corporation, stating the company "hereby makes claim for the value of its tanker the SS *Montebello* ... The undersigned [Stewart] is informed and believes, and therefore states, that as shown by the affidavit of the Master of said ship, Olof W. Ekstrom, hereto attached ... the ship was at the time of sinking within the territorial boundaries of the State of California." Stewart concluded the letter by informing the WDC, "The value of said ship, including cargo and personal property therein, which were lost, was approximately $1,610,000."

The affidavit—attached to Stewart's letter as Exhibit A— subscribed and sworn by Ekstrom—read:

> Olof W. Ekstrom, being first duly swore, deposes and says: That on December 23, 1941, he was the Master and in charge of the S.S. *Montebello*, a tanker belonging to Union Oil Company of California; that at about 5:30 in the morning of that day, while the

ship was proceeding northerly from Port San Luis, California, with a cargo of petroleum products to be delivered at Vancouver, British Columbia, and when the ship was about three and one-half miles from the shoreline near Piedras Blancas Lighthouse, he sighted what he believed to be an enemy submarine. That he immediately commenced to zigzag the ship towards the shore. That about ten minutes later, the ship was struck by a torpedo and soon there-afterwards sank. That at the time of the sinking, according to affiants' best estimate and belief, the ship was within three miles of the coast of the State of California and within the territorial boundaries of that State. That before leaving Port San Luis, affiant was given a clearance by the Navy Department, Twelfth Naval District, at San Francisco, to leave port.

Further affiant saith not.
[Signed] Olof Ekstrom

At this point, Powell's strategy would be to argue two assertions: First, he would contend the loss of the *Montebello* qualified as "the destruction of personal property resulting from enemy action" and therefore covered under the Section 5g amendment to the RFC Act. Second, and of equal or greater importance, he would attempt to prove the tanker, at the time of the sinking, "was situated in the United States and in the State of California, to wit, within three English miles of the shoreline of California."

Ekstrom's affidavit, obtained at Powell's direction, included two small, but significant, details whose importance would be magnified once the trial started. First, the captain, unlike in the interview with E.F. James, now described the zigzag evasive actions taken by the ship as being "toward shore." Second, Ekstrom stated the ship was three and one-half miles from shore when the submarine was first spotted—indicating the combination of factors very likely meant the tanker was sunk "within three English miles of the shoreline of California."

War Damage insurance was to provide "reasonable protection against losses resulting from enemy attacks ... through damage to, or destruction of, buildings, structures, and personal property including goods, growing crops and orchards." The original intent of the insurance, the corporation believed, was to cover common private citizens—to a reasonable monetary amount—for losses such as a farmhouse or barn being destroyed, or a garden or orchard lost to shelling or bombing.

Responding to the Union Oil complaint, filed December 11, 1944, the WDC denied any right of action to recover for the company's loss based on the alleged claims. The corporation would claim that no compensation "was granted or existed" in the provisions of the Reconstruction Finance Act, nor in the amendments to the RFC Act in March 1942. The WDC also denied there was sufficient information to "form a belief as to the truth of the allegation that the *Montebello* ... was situated in the United States, to wit, within three miles of the shoreline of the State of California."

In addition, the WDC had a powerful "Exhibit A" of its own. It possessed a copy of the "Masters Report Regarding the Sinking of the SS *Montebello*" prepared by Olof Ekstrom only a week after the sinking. In the document, the captain stated the ship was approximately *four miles* southwest of the Piedras Blancas Lighthouse and made no mention that the zigzag maneuvers were toward shore. [Italics added.]

Further, the corporation argued the amendments Union Oil cited did not purport to extend the protection to ocean-going ships. "It is evident from the wording of the amendments," the WDC response declared, "that a plan for the protection of American shipping was not contemplated, but that the amendments were concerned with land losses ... the words convey no other meaning."

"The plaintiff makes the argument in its brief that 1) personal property is a broad term which includes ships, and 2) the enumeration in the announcement of personal property excluded from protection did not include ships as an exclusion item, and therefore ships should be deemed included."

The only argument, contended the WDC, which the plaintiff

was able to make was that if an American ship happened to be within the three mile limit, "as is alleged to be the case with the *Montebello,* it is technically personal property in the Continental United States. Surely, there would be no sense in a[n] [insurance] plan which would afford an American ship-owner whose vessel was making a 3,000-mile voyage protection for that minute part of the voyage within three miles of the coast and no protection for the rest of the voyage—perhaps 2,994 miles." The WDC requested its motion to dismiss Union Oil's complaint be granted.

The United States District Court denied the WDC request to dismiss the case. The lawsuit was based on a factual determination; Union Oil alleging that the Montebello was sunk within the three-mile limit. Was the claim correct or not? A jury would be necessary to determine the answer.

This case was going to trial. The lawsuit, Union Oil Company of California vs. War Damage Corporation, would be scheduled for the United States District Court in San Francisco.

Chapter Twelve

The Trial

Nearly five years after the attack and sinking of the *Montebello*, the plaintiff Union Oil Company braced to square off in court against the defendant War Damage Corporation. The case was scheduled to be tried at the Federal Court Building on Seventh Street.

The attorney representing the United States government's War Damage Corporation was Allan Charles from the San Francisco law firm of Lillick, Geary, Olson, and Charles. Assisting him would be Edward Ransom and William Brainerd, young attorneys from the same firm. The plaintiff's representative was Jeremiah Harrison Powell, with assistance from lawyer Paul Sandmeyer.

Charles and Powell could hardly have been more different. Charles grew up in Palo Alto, California, two blocks from Stanford University. Powell had been born and raised in the rural Kentucky town of Richmond. Charles's mother and father were both attorneys themselves; his mother, Isabel, had graduated from Stanford Law School—a rarity for a woman of that time. Powell's father had been a farm laborer in his twenties. Later, he worked for a telephone

Attorney Allan Charles represented the U.S. government.

company. Charles was forty-two years old at the time of the trial while Powell was nearly fifty-seven. Charles, a family man, was married to a fellow Stanford alum; Powell was a bachelor.

The only trait the two lawyers appeared to have shared were bright legal minds. Allan Charles, following both his own interest and family tradition, had graduated from Stanford Law and quickly built a successful practice in San Francisco. Jerry Powell would be the first college-bound member of his family; he had left home to attend Michigan. In 1915, he moved to Los Angeles and began what would become a thriving law practice.

Unlike the sinking of the *Montebello,* which was front-page news across the United States, press coverage of the trial was almost nonexistent. United Press wire stories ran in only a few newspapers, and most of those were in California.

On September 12, 1946, the *San Francisco Examiner* published a brief article in the morning's edition. Buried on page 7, the two-inch story appeared below the small headline declaring: "U.S. TRIAL OPENS IN TORPEDOING."

"The opening of the trial before Federal Judge Michael J. Roche marked the first time that details of an offshore Pacific sinking had been revealed in open court. The [Union Oil] company owned the tanker *Montebello* which was torpedoed and sunk by a submarine three miles off the California coast on December 23, 1941."

"The first witness, Capt. Olof W. Ekstrom, skipper of the *Montebello,* said that gunfire was heard several hours after the ship left San Luis Obispo harbor for Vancouver, B.C. Subsequently, a submarine was sighted and the vessel was torpedoed. Captain Ekstrom and the crew escaped in lifeboats and were picked up later by rescue vessels."

The U.S. Federal Courthouse in San Francisco, where the trial took place.

The weather was a cool fifty-five degrees in San Francisco that morning as the *Montebello* trial began. Along Seventh Street, people in business suits and overcoats hustled about to their offices and shops. Some, though, climbed the few steps into Federal Court Building. There were attorneys, witnesses, jurors, even a few news reporters. They settled into the courtroom as pre-trial tension rose. Papers were shuffled, nervous whispers shared, glances to the opposition made. Finally, the bailiff entered and announced, "All rise." Judge Roche took his seat at the bench. Court was now in session.

Jerry Powell began the proceedings with his opening statement

for the plaintiff. Allan Charles followed for the defendant. Both
opening statements lasted nearly an hour as the lawyers presented
their version of the facts. Both claimed the evidence of witnesses,
expert testimony, and documents would establish the validity of
their claims. Once opening statements were concluded, the lawyers began questioning witnesses.

Captain Olof Ekstrom was first to take the stand. Powell, representing Union Oil, began with a series of questions to illustrate
the extensive experience of the Captain and his record of competence. The jury heard of Ekstrom's training, positions served
aboard ships, and his length of time as a shipmaster. Olof made
a favorable impression with his calm demeanor and confident
responses. He was, in fact, a respected shipmaster. Powell knew
the location of the vessel's sinking—within three miles of the California coast—would be critical and he moved quickly to establish
this as "fact" in the mind of the jury with his questions:

Q. In your judgment, how far were you from the coast at the
time you sighted the submarine, approximately?
A. Well, I would say about three miles off.

Q. In your judgment, approximately how far from the coast
were you at the time your ship was struck by the torpedo?
A. I should say approximately three miles.

Q. Well, were you the same distance from the coast at the time
the torpedo struck you that you were when you first sighted the
submarine? I believe you stated [earlier] when you sighted the
submarine you were approximately three miles from shore.
A. Approximately.

Q. Did you state that you then zigzagged toward the shore?
A. I zigzagged toward the shore, yes.

Q. Had you made any progress toward the shore when you

were struck by the torpedo?

A. I must have done some, yes.

Q. Will you estimate approximately how far you had gone toward the shore?

A. Well, having zigzagged, I can't tell exactly, but I made three-quarters of a mile or so toward shore.

Q. Then am I to understand that when you sighted the submarine you were approximately three miles from the shore?

A. Yes, three miles. I figured I was approximately zigzagging toward shore about three-quarters of a mile.

Powell's repetition of the testimony was a clear effort to ingrain the "inside three miles" testimony with jurors. Through his questions, Powell had placed the *Montebello* almost as close as two miles from shore. When Allan Charles began his cross-examination of Ekstrom, he would attempt to create some measure of "juror doubt" to this claim. He zeroed in on the series of evasive zigzag maneuvers described by the captain.

Q. Which wing [of the bridge] were you on after the submarine was sighted?

A. Well, I was on both sides, off and on, on one side and then the other.

Q. Let's go back to the point where you gave the order that you believe was hard right first. Now, about how long did you have the helmsman hold the hard right rudder before you gave him another order?

A. Well, maybe two or three minutes; less than that.

Q. I know it is difficult to ask you to remember all the details under the excitement that existed at the time, but I was wondering if you could recall whether you had formulated any plan in your mind about that zigzagging; did you intend to hold to that right rudder long enough to get your stern off the original course, or did you have in mind swinging back in the other direction before your stern had a chance to get off the original course?

A. Well, of course, the stern, when I say, "Hard right" and go full speed the ship will start swinging.

Q. She would start swinging right away?
A. Slowly, and then increase speed as she goes in.

Q. But it would take two or three minutes before her stern would get off that original course, even at full speed, wouldn't it?
A. No, I wouldn't say—off her regular course, I wouldn't say that long, because the whole ship swings together.

Q. Yes, but she would go four or five ship lengths, wouldn't she, Captain, before the stern would really get off that original course to the right? Do you see what I mean?
A. Yes, but if you look at the wake of a ship when it swings, the minute she starts swinging the wake will have a curve in it; the stern will swing at the same time.

Q. But to get your stern over to the right of your original course will take a couple of minutes, won't it, under those conditions?
A. I don't understand what you mean.

Q. Let me explain this: If you want to turn as fast as you can to the right—
A. Yes.

Q. You give your helmsman a hard right rudder order, don't you?
A. Yes.

Q. The first thing that happens is that your stern moves off a little bit to the left as your bow moves to the right?

A. Yes.

Q. Your bow keeps swinging to the right?

A. Yes.

Q. About how far would your ship go forward in the water before the stern, which has moved a little to the left of your course, gets over the right angle and starts to pull away from that original course?

A. A stern would swing at the same moment as the bow swings.

Q. Yes, that is true, but how long does it take before that gets off the line of your original course?

A. That is something I never figured out.

Charles had spotlighted an important question to the jury: How long would a hard right turn need to be held before the ship leaves its previous course? If such an order was followed too quickly by a hard left order, the vessel would not have progressed toward shore at all. Charles now pressed that very issue.

Q. Your best recollection is after you held her hard right about two minutes or less you then gave the order, "Hard left"?

A. Yes.

Q. Have you any recollection about how long you held that hard left rudder?

A. Well, it was only a very, very short time.

Q. Then do you recall whether you got another rudder order in before you got [hit by] the torpedo?

A. Yes, I had several.

Q. Several more?

A. In ten minutes' time I had several maneuvers in there to the rudder.

Q. Do you recall whether or not you alternated more or less to the right or to the left?
A. I alternated more to the right.

Q. More rudder orders to the right than to the left?
A. Yes. I wanted to get in closer to the coast in case I get sunk.

Q. But you did not hold her on a right rudder for a long time? I mean you did not make any right-angle turn, or anything like that?
A. No. I would turn clear around that way.

The War Damage Corporation's attorney had succeeded. How could zigzagging be performed without alternating turns? In hindsight, Captain Ekstrom seemed to have erred in testifying he'd made more right-rudder orders. Charles believed he had chipped away at the distance-from-shore testimony. As the trial continued, he knew his team would need to *blast* it away.

Soon it was Edward Ransom's turn. Charles's colleague sought to further damage the "three mile" Union Oil assertion as he questioned Daniel Seed, the *Montebello's* 1st assistant engineer.

Q. How did you leave the ship then, what direction did the lifeboat go?
A. We rowed around to our left and went under the stern of the ship, heading to shore.

Q. Did you see the *Montebello* sink?
A. I did.

Q. Do you know about what time she sank?
A. Approximately ten minutes to seven.

Q. How do you know that?
A. By my wristwatch.

Q. Was it dark at that time?
A. It was getting light by that time.

Q. What could you see of the *Montebello* when she sank?
A. You could see the whole ship; she went down slowly by the bow.

Q. You could see it clearly?
A. I could see her very clearly.

Q. By that time could you see the shoreline?
A. Yes; I saw the mountains, which is the shoreline, the mountains come right directly up to it.

Q. Do you know what direction the *Montebello* was heading?
A. In a general northwesterly direction.

Q. Could you see the breakers at any time?
A. No, we could not.

Q. In your approximately twenty years at sea up to that time, what experience had you had in measuring distances?
A. Well, the same as anybody else that is looking for the shoreline and figuring what time he is going to get home, being on the deck when you approach the land.

Q. Did you form any estimate of the distance your small boat was from the *Montebello* at the time the *Montebello* sank?
A. Yes, I did.

Q. What would you estimate that distance to be?
A. Between one and one-half and two miles.

Q. The small boat was between the *Montebello* and the shore, is that your testimony?

A. That's right.

Q. Did you form any estimate at the time the *Montebello* sank of the distance from your lifeboat to the land?

A. Yes, I did.

Q. What was the distance?

A. Between three and one-half and four miles; maybe a little over.

Q. Having estimated the distance between your boat and the *Montebello,* and your boat and the shore, what did you estimate the distance the *Montebello* was from the shore at the time she sank?

A. Five miles, maybe a little over; between five and six, I would say.

Seed's testimony had shaken Union Oil's claim that the ship was sunk within the territorial limits—and given the jury a very different mileage figure to consider. Ransom's examination, and Seed's responses, had succeeded in shifting the balance of belief; the issue of the *Montebello's* distance to shore was now in question.

The following day, Union Oil's Paul Sandmeyer attempted to repair the company's position by re-calling Olof Ekstrom to the stand. The Captain described in detail the final sailing of the *Montebello,* up to and including, the attack. Ekstrom again asserted the ship was close to shore when she sunk.

"I believe," he said, "the vessel went down, checking on the course and speed, at least when she was hit, she was approximately one and-one-half miles to two miles from the shoreline, to the best of my recollection."

Sandmeyer called the captain forward to a display board of the coastline where the *Montebello* was attacked. The large map depicted Union Oil's location at the point of attack and place of sinking—marked by letters. Sandmeyer intended to show the ship sank within the territorial waters of California and plunged directly down rather than gliding away from shore as she sank.

Q. How long a time, in your estimate, passed between the time you saw the submarine until the torpedo struck, that is, the explosion?

A. Approximately ten or fifteen minutes.

Q. Captain, when the vessel was sunk, I believe you said it went down by the bow first. I wonder if you could describe to the jury how the vessel sank?

A. When the vessel was torpedoed she settled down almost immediately on the fore part, and then she settled gradually more and more, and by the time she went down, the after end of the vessel came up about 150 feet in the air, and then she went straight down.

Q. That is, the after end of the vessel was vertical to the surface of the water and she went straight down?

A. She went straight down.

Q. I believe you said you were about five hundred feet away, or five hundred yards?

A. Approximately five or six hundred feet away.

Q. Did I understand you to say this morning that the distance where she sunk was one and one-half to two miles from the shoreline?

A. Approximately. It might have been more, it might have been less.

Q. That would be approximately where this Point H is [indicating]?

A. Approximately. She was torpedoed at Point H.

The witness was passed to the defendant's attorney. During cross-examination with the captain, Allan Charles reached a pivotal issue in the testimony: Ekstrom's recollection of the ship's distance from shore was now significantly different from his statements immediately after the sinking in 1941 and from his sworn deposition in 1945. Charles asked the captain if he was aware of the importance of the accurate location of a wreck being given to the United States Navy for its "wreck list."

Q. [Charles]. …and there is a statement in that wreck list that the position of the wreck is given so that the vessels of the United States won't be depth bombing their own wrecks?
A. That position on the chart where the ship went down is placed approximately. If you take a chart of the Atlantic Coast, a wreck chart where thousands of ships were torpedoed on the Atlantic Coast during this war, there isn't one in the correct position.

Q. I do not want to argue with you on that. There probably isn't one of them that was torpedoed just a few miles from her port of departure. What I am asking—and I don't want to quarrel with you—is just this thing: You do know, don't you, that the location of the wreck of a ship in time of war, when our vessels are looking for an enemy submarine, is and was of vital importance?
A. The Navy Intelligence and the Army Intelligence no doubt know where the vessel was.

Q. Why would they know where it was other than from your testimony?
A. At that time when the vessel was sunk we were at war and everything was a military secret. There was no person outside of myself that was supposed to know where that vessel was. That was a military secret. It wasn't supposed it be given out. The Navy and Army Intelligence—it was their business to know exactly if that

vessel was a menace to navigation, which they probably did know two hours after the vessel went down.

Q. Captain, I wasn't asking you about a danger to navigation. I was asking you if you did not realize the importance of the position with respect to the danger that the ship would be depth bombed under the misbelief that it was as enemy craft, an enemy submarine?

A. You couldn't depth bomb that thing, because there was no sound from it.

Q. You are familiar with the fact that her wreck list position...

A. I am familiar with submarines; they never depth-bomb wrecks.

Q. And also there is an explicit direction in the wreck list to use care, or a definite statement in the wreck list that the place of these wrecks is given so that the navy will not be led astray in the bombing of their own wrecks in the belief that they are submarines?

A. It can't be done. Why should we bomb our own wrecks? They are submerged, no noise, and no way to detect.

Q. I will get that wreck list statement and show it to you, Captain. At the time that you made that statement, "four miles off," you believed it to be correct, didn't you?

A. As far as I did, yes.

The Union Oil team had tried its best to stop the trial from hemorrhaging, but Powell and Sandmeyer knew they had a serious problem. The next day would bring more testimonial trouble, this time coming in the form of a lightkeeper and two marine geophysicists.

Chapter Thirteen

Gun flashes, Scientists, and a Verdict

As the trial began its fifth day, attorneys for Union Oil and War Damage Corporation had made persuasive arguments before the court. In testimony the previous day, Charles, a specialist in maritime law, had prompted an important concession from Olof Ekstrom—that on the morning of the attack, the *Montebello*, had been an estimated four miles off shore. On Day Five Charles planned to call witnesses and experts to the stand to provide testimony that, he hoped, would tilt the scales of advantage strongly in his favor.

Norman Francis, the lightkeeper at Piedras Blancas, was called to testify. He had been interviewed by both legal teams a year before at the light station. But during their visit, the War Damage team had seized on a piece of information that would prove vitally important during the trial: rocks.

The morning of the attack, Francis and his assistant Joseph Harrington had positioned themselves at the base of the light tower looking in a southerly direction. Through the dark, both men had seen the gun flashes as the *I-21* fired at the *Montebello*.

Later, Francis realized the flashes had appeared directly above a set of rocks, perhaps twenty-five feet in height, on the station property. Allan Charles and his team knew that an engineer, armed with a surveying instrument called a "transit," used to measure horizontal angles and precise directions, could determine a probable line upon which the *Montebello* wreck might be located. This was a strategy they quietly hoped to exploit to full advantage.

Back in federal court, Charles began to lay the foundation for "locating" the ship. He presented questions to Francis about his observations the morning of the attack.

Q. Would you go on and tell the jury in your own words what, if anything, you observed?

A. At the time I was standing at the base of the tower facing in a southerly direction.

Q. Could I ask you about what time that was?

A. That was about 5:30 AM, as I remember it, when I observed a gun flashing. At that time the visibility was quite obscured by moderate rain, so that visibility at that time probably was only about a half a mile. However, this gun flash that I saw flashed out in the rain. About the time that I saw it two or three other men with me observed it also. We stood looking in that direction, and we observed two more flashes, gunfire. That was all, though. There wasn't anything else visible but the gun flashes. At that time, I unconsciously made a note of the direction, and I estimated in discussing with the men just about how far out these gun flashes were—we thought it was about five miles. That was just guessing due to the reduced visibility caused by the rain. We couldn't hear the explosions of the gun, as at that time the wind was blowing quite brisk from the northwest, so that it would have carried the sound of gunfire away from the station.

Q. Do you recall, Mr. Francis, an engineer by the name of Parker Palmer calling upon you with a transit about a year ago?

A. Yes.

Q. Did you at that time make any effort to show him the direction in which you had seen the gun flashes?

A. Yes, I had. They asked me and I helped them, and I gave the position as I remembered it. Before I go further, there was a rock sticking out twenty or thirty feet high above the bluff below the light in that direction which I was facing, and I used that as a [reference] point.

Q. Had you observed the gunfire with relation to that rock?

A. Well, at the time I hadn't, but I subconsciously sort of, later on, made up my mind that the rock was in line, and I sort of subconsciously noted that.

Upon cross-examination, Union Oil's Sandmeyer immediately seized on Francis's "subconscious" recollection of the rock formation and pressed him on it. He suggested the recollection was a rather convenient one.

Q. Mr. Francis, your last testimony was that four and a half years ago when you were looking at those flashes you did not line the flashes up with any particular point, that is correct, isn't it?

A. No, not at that time, no, I hadn't taken any particular point of them concerning the rock.

Q. It was only later that you recalled you had seen the lights out in that direction and sort of lined up the flashes being somewhere along where that rock was, is that correct?

A. That came into my mind that I had observed the rock, like I explained, subconsciously.

Q. You recall after two or three years that you saw this rock out in a south-southeast direction?

A. Yes, that's right.

Q. The point I am making is, you testified, both on direct and in answer to my question that at the time you saw the flashes you did not line them up with the rock?

A. Naturally I didn't at the time, because lots of times you don't pay attention to observations, but unconsciously those details register later on, so that is part of my work, to make observations, and probably I don't pay much attention at the time.

Sandmeyer had damaged the credibility of Francis's testimony; the explanation that "unconsciously-those-details-register" appeared questionable to nearly everyone in the court.

Regardless of how that testimony may have resonated, Allan Charles knew something others in the courtroom did not: Francis's rock alignment had merit.

The lightkeeper's granite rock reference point had given Charles and the WDC an ace-in-the-hole.

On September 18, the WDC presented two witnesses who the corporation had hired in 1945 to pull off something that would seem to have been next to impossible given the technology of the time: find and photograph the wreck of the *Montebello* hundreds of feet below the ocean's surface.

Fran Shepard was a highly regarded marine geologist from Scripps Institution of Oceanography in California. Partnering with him was twenty-one-year-old John Ewing of Woods Hole Oceanographic Institute in Massachusetts.[13]

Virtually everyone in the courtroom leaned forward with attentive ears as Ewing presented both scientist's findings. He testified that they'd begun their search for the *Montebello* aboard a Coast Guard cutter loaned to the WDC.

They combed the ocean surface along the longitudinal lines derived from Norman Francis's rock description and the engineer's transit. Ewing and Shepard quickly discovered oil bubbling to the surface where the depth of the water was approximately 800 feet. Due to water currents below the surface, they were unsure if the oil they'd found had originated from a source directly below.

But the two scientists knew technology that might have surprised lay people of the times. They began mapping the area with echo sounders that transmitted an acoustic wave into the water. Ewing and Shepard then analyzed the return signals and soon discovered a large object they believed to be a ship on the ocean floor at a depth slightly less than 900 feet.

The equipment used by the scientists to take underwater photographs was primitive by today's standards. Ewing was required to make dozens of exhausting attempts to sink an underwater camera in position to obtain images of the wreck. He was able to take only one exposure with each effort before hauling the waterproof casing—and the camera within—back to the surface and changing the flash.

Despite the challenging conditions, he successfully photographed portions of the ship. Though the scientists were unable to confirm it was the *Montebello,* the images Ewing had captured revealed the ship's unique deck arrangement of pipes, valves, and hold covers. Only one other vessel existed that matched the exact characteristics of the *Montebello*: her sister-ship *La Placentia.*

The WDC team then located and photographed the *La Placentia,* moored in Martinez, California. Shots of the tanker were compared to images of the wreck off San Simeon taken by Ewing. The deck equipment of the two vessels matched perfectly.

Ewing's testimony, of course, damaged Union Oil's case as if it were a torpedo itself, ripping a hole in Ekstrom's "about three miles" claim. The shipwreck discovered by the marine scientists was, beyond question, the *Montebello.*

Even more devastating, the location of the wreck was over *six* miles off the California coast, contrary to Union's claim, and well beyond the territorial waters of the United States.

The impact of the new evidence was overwhelming. Ewing and Shepard's findings had blasted the "within territorial limits" scenario to pieces.

The *Montebello* had been found; the echo-location and

photographic proof linking the sister ships was indisputable.

Allan Charles and his team had saved their best for last and proven, it seemed, beyond all reasonable doubt, the tanker's actual distance from shore—the critical "disputed fact" upon which the case hinged. And everyone in the courtroom knew it.

With the appropriate demeanor of reserved expressions and quiet resolve, the War Damage Corporation team ended the proceedings that day straightening files on the desktop and placed them in their briefcases.

They knew better than to be overconfident in predicting a winning verdict from a jury. They'd have to wait until the next day.

But deep inside, they liked their chances.

The thin veil of fog over the city disappeared early the final day of the trial. That Friday, temperatures reached a Death Valley-like ninety degrees—beyond scorching for mild San Francisco. The outcome of the *Montebello* case seemed to have cleared, too.

Attorneys for both sides gave their closing arguments. The War Damage team's statement was a concise summation of the testimony—with emphasis on the evidence presented by the marine scientists the previous day. Shepard and Ewing had strengthened the WDC case like reinforced concrete.

By contrast, the Union Oil attorneys faced an impossible position to defend. Nevertheless, they tried. They attempted to argue that the ship had sunk within three miles of the coast but had moved through years of bottom currents and a sloped sea floor before coming to rest in its present location.[14] Few, if any, gave the explanation any credence.

Judge Roche advised the jury, "a corporation is entitled to the same fair trial as a private individual," before directing them to chambers for deliberations.

The length of jury discussions—like a weather sock—can be an indicator of the direction the legal winds have blown: toward victory or defeat. This day, the deliberations were short.

When the jurors re-entered the courtroom, Judge Roche asked,

"Has the jury reached a verdict?" Indeed, they had. The decision was handed to the judge who announced the findings to the courtroom.

Union Oil had lost its war-claim suit.

Allan Charles and his team had convinced the jury the tanker was, in fact, sunk outside territorial waters, therefore exempting the government from any responsibility. Under the law, Union Oil was due no compensation.

With the conclusion of the trial, the story of the *Montebello* had closed.

Or had it?

Chapter Fourteen

Rediscovered

For the next fifty-one years, the *Montebello* lay undisturbed on the ocean bottom off Cambria and San Simeon. Over time, the story of her sinking receded into the vague realm of Central Coast lore and remained largely forgotten outside a few fishermen, museum docents, and locals with an interest in history.

That changed rapidly with the establishment of the Monterey Bay National Marine Sanctuary in 1992. Soon, the *Montebello* again became a topic of interest, though not for her historical significance. She now presented a potentially serious environmental hazard. Over three million gallons of crude oil could still be aboard and therefore posing the quandary of what—if anything—should be done.

The *Montebello* wasn't an isolated ecological threat. In the summer of 1953, the 469-foot freighter SS *Luckenbach* collided with her sister ship the SS *Hawaiian Pilot*. The *Luckenbach* sank in 178 feet of water near the Farallon Islands only seventeen miles off San Francisco. After decades at the bottom of the sea, oil began leaking through the ship's corroded ventilation pipes. Dozens of oil spills, all mysteriously emanating from the same location, at first went unrecognized by officials as traceable to the sunken freighter.

The amount of oil spill increased significantly when Pacific storms rocked the shipwreck. Oil rose to the surface and, over time, killed more than fifty-one thousand seabirds. The California Department of Fish and Game performed chemistry analysis that confirmed the oil spills and bird deaths were clearly linked to the *Luckenbach*. Tar balls were discovered from Bodega Bay to Monterey Bay—a distance in excess of 130 nautical miles. Again, the tar was linked chemically to the ship. Cleanup of the *Luckenbach* would eventually cost $20 million.

With this context, concern grew from environmentalists who argued that the *Montebello* could pose a similarly destructive threat to the waters and wildlife of the sanctuary—and beyond. The shipwreck began getting governmental attention. Efforts to assess and prevent a *Luckenbach*-like environmental mess gained momentum and focus.

The first wreck-site investigations, conducted by the National Oceanic and Atmospheric Administration (NOAA), involved launching a manned submersible to the site in 1996. Those expeditions confirmed the findings of Fran Shepard and John Ewing, the marine geologists who made the initial discovery in 1945. The *Montebello's* location was, indeed, well beyond the three-mile territorial waters. The tanker was found six miles off the coast of Cambria and eight miles south of Piedras Blancas Light Station at a depth of 885 feet. Attorney Allan Charles and the War Damage Corporation, it turned out, had not only argued successfully, but correctly.

The 1996 NOAA team included archaeologist and project director Jack Hunter, archaeologist Roy Pettus, biologist Stacy Kim, and historian Robert Schwemmer. The investigation provided the first survey of the *Montebello* wreck and obtained information to help evaluate the environmental threat it might pose.

The team, aboard the support vessel *Cavalier*, launched the deep-sea submersible *Delta* for four dives to the wreck. They found the ship covered in a spider web of fishing nets. Their observations

Location of the *Montebello* sinking.

revealed the hull to be well preserved with no immediate signs
of deterioration. No evidence of impending leakage of oil was
noted. Also documented at the site was an abundance of fish and
invertebrate life on, and around, the wreck. The ship had become,
in essence, an underwater oasis in an otherwise flat sandy seabed.

The *Montebello* was sitting upright on the seafloor as if tied to
a dock. "It was not until the end of the fourth reconnaissance dive
that the bow section was located," the Department of Fish and
Game report stated. "It was discovered that the cutwater was buried in the sand [approximately thirty feet] ahead of the main hull,
with the aftermost part of the bow rising above the sea floor at a
40-degree angle with a slight list to port."

This led the team to conclude that, upon sinking, the *Monte-bello* had struck the ocean floor with enough force for the section of the bow at the torpedo strike-point to sheer off and embed in the flat sand plain. The hull damage from the warhead's explosive impact was plainly visible with an arc of shredded steel plates.

The remaining 90 percent of the ship recoiled upon impact, the team believed, and settled upright on the bottom. The investigation conclusively indicated that the torpedo had struck the ship forward of the oil storage tanks and penetrated the pump room in the dry storage hold.

Hunter and Schwemmer would again be part of a 2003 marine sanctuary science study, this time aboard the research vessel *Velero IV*. Eight dives to the *Montebello* were made in the *Delta* submersible over a two-day period. The team's mission was to determine if signs of oil discharge were present and if there was evidence of Beggiatoa bacteria feeding on hydrocarbons—an indicator that marine environments had been subject to pollution. Neither was found. Some degradation was noted in steel hull plates since the 1996 expedition.

In 2009, California Assemblyman Sam Blakeslee became aware of the *Montebello*'s worrisome potential and initiated a risk assessment to determine the likelihood of an oil release and the potential adverse effects such a scenario could cause. The *Monte-bello* Assessment Task Force was formed.

Two years later, Global Diving and Salvage, Inc. was awarded a Coast Guard contract to determine if oil was present on the sunken ship. The M/V *Nanuq* conducted a survey of the site using a remotely operated vehicle, or ROV. The ROV was equipped to conduct ultrasonic thickness gauging of the steel hull and to determine if oil was present in the tanks.

To accomplish these tasks, the ROV first cleaned portions of the *Montebello*'s hull, then used ultrasound to measure the thickness of the metal plates.

"Once that's done, then we bring in the nuclear tool, which is

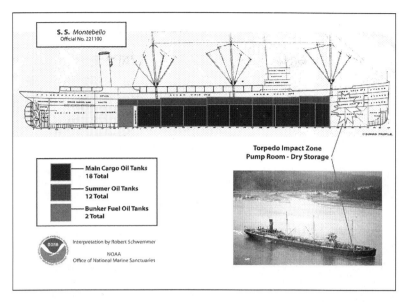

Diagram of oil tanks and location of torpedo strike. (Design credit: Robert Schwemmer/NOAA Office of National Marine Sanctuaries)

a diagnostic scan device," said Kerry Walsh, the project manager. "We press that up against the hull and measure through the steel, and we can detect by the return signal from the neutron backscatter what's behind it. You get one kind of signal if it is seawater, and another kind of signal if it is oil."

In October 2011, the Coast Guard Report concluded that no substantial oil threat existed to California waters and shorelines. "Neutron backscatter analysis, a non-destructive technology that helps determine the probability of oil within the tanks, was performed," said the report. "Sediment samples were also collected from the area surrounding the vessel yielding no evidence of oil contamination. Tank samples have been drawn and visual inspection indicates there is no quantifiable amount of oil onboard."

A request was made to have tests performed on coupons—small cores of metal removed from the hull of the ship—to determine the overall corrosion rate. It was the opinion of Engineering Systems Inc. (2012) that the wreck of the Montebello will maintain on-site

**The MV *Nanuq* launching an ROV to examine the *Montebello's* hull, 2011.
(National Oceanic and Atmospheric Administration)**

stability for many decades to come.

All of which leads to the question: where did the oil go?

NOAA scientists considered a number of hypothetical release scenarios and simulated computer trajectory models for each. "Given the data discovered and records available, a long-term release model seems most reasonable," said NOAA Scientific Support Coordinator Jordan Stout. "Such a model indicates that most of the oil remained offshore and headed south, some would have evaporated within the first few days, and the remainder may have washed ashore but may have been so widely scattered it went unnoticed. There are a number of unknowns associated with this release; therefore, we will probably never know exactly what happened to the oil."

There are times in life when a mystery remains a mystery. The disappearance of the oil, however it occurred, means the SS

Montebello poses no environment concern. To the contrary, the ship now functions as an artificial reef in the deep waters off the California shoreline and is home to a thriving array of sea life.

But with the oil threat gone, and the tanker hidden beneath the depths of the Pacific, the importance of the *Montebello* could, once again, become a forgotten footnote of California's past.

It shouldn't.

The ship represents the history and importance of the oil tanker in peacetime and war. The fuel required to warm houses, power engines, and, in times of conflict, enable the defense of democracy, was transported—lest we forget—upon vessels built and sailed by men.

The story of the *Montebello* is a reminder of a pivotal time in our history—a time when America was attacked not only in the distant waters at Pearl Harbor, but directly along her own continental shores. Today, few people are aware that enemy submarines marauded along the U.S. Pacific Coast during the early months of World War II. The *Montebello* remains a powerful witness to those perilous days. Her loss, and the loss of other ships like her, forced Americans to recognize that war might not always be fought in faraway lands and could arrive suddenly in their own front yard.

But the *Montebello* is also a story of people. A reminder of a crew that knowingly sailed into harm's way. Of a captain who, in the words of one crewman, remained "as cool as a snowdrift" while under attack. And of citizens who leaped into action at a moment's notice, people in Cambria rallying to rescue survivors.

Said the poet Ralph Waldo Emerson: "What lies behind us and what lies before us are tiny matters compared to what lies within us."

That quiet voice which can answer a long-foreseen call of duty, or respond in an instant to its quick appearance; the stowaway in the human heart that can rise to the forefront in the midst of a tempest.

Epilogue

Olof Ekstrom: Four months after the sinking of the SS *Montebello,* Ekstrom received the Maritime Eagle Decoration of Honor for his "outstanding conduct" in the American merchant marine service. He continued as master of Union Oil tankers. After retiring, Olof, and wife Olga, moved to San Diego. He died there in 1963 at age sixty-eight.

Mogens Andreasen: The Danish-born shipmaster retired in 1945 after a forty-four year career at sea. Mogens and his wife Martine lived in San Francisco for the remainder of their lives. He died in 1973 at the age of ninety-two.

Allan Charles: The San Francisco attorney continued his successful law practice until his retirement in 1975. He died in his sleep at his home in San Francisco on November 8, 1999. He was ninety-six. In the *San Francisco Chronicle* obituary, only one of his cases received mention—the *Montebello* trial that he'd won for the federal government.

Jerry Powell: Jeremiah Harrison Powell practiced law for nearly fifty years. Three years after the trial, Powell spearheaded another claim for Union Oil involving the sinking of the ship. This one was based on the War Claims Act passed by Congress in 1948. The Act allowed for compensation of prisoners of war and authorized reparations for war damage and loss. Funds for the program were generated from the sale of Japanese and German assets seized by the United States after World War II. Powell's actions resulted in a $629,000 award to Union Oil from the U.S. Treasury. Powell died in Los Angeles on September 18, 1960 at the age of seventy.

SS Larry Doheny: On the evening of October 5, 1942, the *Larry Doheny*'s luck would run out. The ship was attacked by the Japanese submarine *I-25* thirty-six miles off the southern coast of Oregon. Six Americans were killed. The vessel's forty survivors were rescued by the USS *Coos Bay*. The ship sank the following day in 4,500 feet of water.

Kanji Matsumura: The Japanese commander served aboard the *I-21* until March 16, 1943 when he was assigned as an instructor in the navy's submarine school. In September 1944, he joined the submarine *I-177* and was assigned a patrol near the Palau Islands. On the evening of October 1, 1944, he was among 101 Japanese sailors who died when *I-177* was sunk by the U.S. destroyer *Samuel B. Miles*. Captain Matsumura was promoted two ranks to Vice-Admiral, posthumously.

Alma: The *Alma* has carried a degree of honor since the December day her crew plucked survivors from *Montebello* lifeboats miles off the coast and returned them safely to the Cayucos wharf. The tug was retired in the mid-1990s and is now a permanent land-based display at the Morro Bay Maritime Museum.

Norman Francis: The officer-in-charge served at Piedras Blancas Light Station until retiring in May 1948. He and his wife Florence eventually settled in San Pedro near the Los Angeles Harbor Lighthouse he had been assigned to as a young man. Norman died in November 1961 at seventy years of age.

Joseph Harrington: The Irish-born thirty-three-year veteran of the United States Lighthouse Service was scheduled to retire within one week of the sinking of the *Montebello*—on December 31, 1941. Nonetheless, Harrington immediately volunteered his services to the government "in any capacity whatever." His offer was accepted and he was again placed on duty at Piedras Blancas. He would serve an additional three years at the light station—retiring finally at age sixty-nine.

John Ewing: Ewing had a long and distinguished career in

marine geophysical research. He retired from Woods Hole in 1989. Over the course of his career, he received numerous awards, among them the prestigious Francis P. Shepard Medal—named in honor of the project partner with whom Ewing mapped and photographed the wreck of the *Montebello* in 1945. Ewing died in 2001 at age seventy-seven.

John Ewing

Japanese Submarine I-21: Soon after sinking the *Montebello*, the I-21 was assigned to patrol off the East Coast of Australia. Over the next seventeen months, the submarine sank eight ships and severely damaged two others. In March of 1943 Commander Inada Hiroshi replaced the highly successful but now re-assigned Kanji Matsumura aboard the *I-21*. The submarine's last radio report was sent on November 27, 1943, southwest of Tarawa. Two days later, torpedo-bombers found and sunk a submarine believed to be the *I-21*. The boat was never heard from again.

Piedras Blancas Light Station: On December 31, 1948, an earthquake damaged the 100-foot light tower, leading to the removal of the upper landing, watch room, and lantern room. The first-order Fresnel lens was replaced with a 36-inch aerobeacon. Currently, a Vega marine rotating beacon sits atop the now seventy-foot truncated light tower producing a white flash every ten seconds.

The light station was transferred from the Coast Guard to the Bureau of Land Management in October 2001. The Fresnel lens—the same lens that was shining on the morning of the attack on the Montebello—was loaned to the Cambria Lions Club and moved

Piedras Blancas Light Station today.

to an enclosure on Main Street in Cambria where it is on display.

Avila: By the mid-1950s, the quaint seaside community began petitioning local officials to change the name from Avila to Avila Beach. The aged oil storage tanks on the hills above, and pipelines below the streets of Avila, had been leaking for decades, contaminating the soil and groundwater. A lawsuit initiated by the local group "Avila Alliance" prompted a long list of government agencies to become involved. In the late 1990s Union Oil, by then known as Unocal, acknowledged responsibility for the spill.

The company paid $200 million in one of the largest environmental settlements of the time. The clean-up required removal of soil—nearly 7,000 truckloads—and razing most of the town's buildings. The new millennium began with the reconstruction of buildings, homes, businesses, and oceanfront. The town's mild climate, protected beach, and revitalized Front Street have drawn frequent visitors to Avila Beach. Tourism is now the main industry.

One of the few buildings to survive the razing of downtown was the Avila Grocery. Taken apart and later reconstructed, the market sits in its original location on Front Street. Middle Dock was destroyed in a powerful storm in 1983.

No.1 Lifeboat Oar: The oar retrieved by young Frank Goodall remains the only known artifact from the SS *Montebello* to survive the attack. It is on display at the Cambria Historical Society Museum located in Cambria's East Village on Center Street.

SS Montebello: In September 2016, the *Montebello* shipwreck and her remains were added to the National Register of Historic Places—providing additional federal protection for the site. The ship lies just one and one-half miles south of the Monterey Bay Marine Sanctuary.

The oar that young Frank Goodall retrieved from the lifeboat during the rescue.

The *Montebello* rests on a flat seabed only six miles from the beaches of Cambria and San Simeon—and a mere thirty-six nautical miles north of Port San Luis where she began her ill-fated final voyage in December 1941.

References

Miscellaneous information regarding individuals was obtained through hundreds of documents, including ship manifests, birth and death certificates, government appointment logs, military records, school yearbooks, newspaper articles, census records, voter registrations, immigration records, etc. available through on-line search sources. Here are more specific sources for some of the book's more prominent topics:

Andreasen, Mogens
Bethlehem Steel Company, San Pedro, Shipbuilding History. *Union Oil Bulletin*, March, 1933 Volume IX, Bulletin No. 3.
Montebello Building and Service Record
Monterey Bay National Marine Sanctuary, Maritime Heritage: Field Research *Montebello*.
National Achieves, San Bruno Branch, SS *Montebello* file.
National Park Service
National Register of Historic Places Continuation Sheet *Montebello* (shipwreck and remains) Ref. no. 16000636.
SF Gate: Oil Aboard Sunken WWII Tanker May Pose Threat.

The SS *Montebello,* Past Tragedy, Future Disaster by Glen Julian, www.militarymuseum.org.

United States Census Records, Immigration Documents, Public Record.

Ekstrom, Olof

Civil Case #24101, National Archives, San Bruno Branch. *Los Angeles Times* December 24, 1941.

San Pedro News Pilot (San Pedro, California). Volume 15, Number 68, May 23, 1942.

United States Census Records, Immigration Documents, Public Record.

Japanese Submarine I-21

Combined Fleet.com.

IJNsubsite.info. Naval Heritage and History Command www.history.navy.mil.

Militaryfactory.com IJN *I-21* Ocean-Going Diesel-Electric Attack Submarine.

San Francisco Maritime National Park Association www.maritime.org/tech/torpfire.htm.

Larry Doheny, Pacific Typhoon

Honolulu Advertiser (Hawaii), December 9, 1934.

Vancouver Daily Province (Vancouver, B.C.), October 24, 1934.

Long Lance torpedo

Tameichi Hara (1967). *Japanese Destroyer Captain: Pearl Harbor, Guadalcanal, Midway–The Great Naval Battles as Seen Through Japanese Eyes* (F. Saito & R. Pineau, Trans.). Annapolis, MD: Naval Institute Press.

Matsumura, Kanji

Combined Fleet.com.

Historynet.com Japanese Submarines Prowl the U.S. Pacific

Coastline in 1941.

IJNsubsite.info.

Military.wikia.org Japanese Submarine *I-21.*

Militaryfactory.com IJN *I-21* Ocean-Going Diesel-Electric Attack Submarine.

National Park Service. National Register of Historic Places Continuation Sheet *Montebello* (shipwreck and remains) Ref. no. 16000636.

United States Department of the Interior

Montebello, sight survey expeditions

California Department of Fish & Game, Final Press Release October 20, 2011.

California Department of Fish & Game, SS *Montebello* Assessing Potential Pollution Effects to the Marine Environment and California Coast.

Chico Record (Chico), December 23, 1941.

Monterey Bay National Marine Sanctuary, Maritime Heritage: Field Research *Montebello,* SS *Montebello* videos.

NBC News, "World War II Shipwrecks Pose Oil Spill Threat" by Jessica Marshall, July 22, 2011.

NPR's "All Things Considered," Six Miles Offshore: The Wreck of *Montebello,* October 18, 2011.

Oil Spill Task Force Legacy Award 2012 *Montebello* Project. Team, Cpt. Roger LaFerriere, LCDR Angie Hidalgo, LCDR Caryn Margita, LT Lori Loughran, MS Jill Lemon, CWO Michael Jolly, MTSC Jeff Deronde.

Montebello, sinking and other West Coast attacks

California Department of Fish & Wildlife, *Montebello* Timeline.

Californian (Salinas), December 24, 1941.

HistoryNet.com.

Lompoc Record, December 26, 1941.

Los Angeles Times December 23, 1941.

Los Angeles Times, December 24, 1941.

National Archives Quarterly, Prologue Vol. 23 No.3.

News-Pilot (San Pedro), December 22, 1941.

Santa Cruz Evening News, December 23, 1941.

News-Pilot (San Pedro), December 24, 1941.

Santa Maria Daily Times, December 23, 1941.

Silent Siege-III by Bert Webber.

Staff Ride Handbook for the attack on Pearl Harbor, December 7, 1941: a study of defending America / LTC Jeffrey J. Gudmens and the Staff Ride Team, Combat Studies Institute Press, June 2009.

Vancouver Daily Province (Vancouver, B.C.), December 24, 1941.

Ventura County Star Free-Press, December 22, 1941.

Visalia Times December 23, 1941.

Montebello, wreck discovery

American Institute of Physics interview with John and Betty Ewing, May 21, 1996.

California Department of Fish & Wildlife, Data Portal, S.S. *Montebello*: Assessing potential pollution effects to the marine environment and California coast. (Undated).National Park Service

https://nmsmontereybay.blob.core.windows.net/monterey-bay-prod/media/maritime/images/ss*Montebello* _chp3.mov.

National Marine Sanctuaries and NOAA video series on the *Montebello* expeditions and discovery.

National Register of Historic Places Continuation Sheet *Montebello* (shipwreck and remains) Ref. no. 16000636.

Political climate, 1941 understanding of

Truman by David McCullough, Simon and Schuster, 1992.

Port and towns, 1941 descriptions of (Port San Luis, Cayucos, Cambria, San Simeon, and Piedras Blancas)

United States Coast Pilot, 1942, Sixth Edition.

Rescue
The Cambrian, December 25, 1941 and January 1, 1942.
Civil Case #24101, National Archives, San Bruno Branch.
Los Angeles Times, December 24, 1941.
National Park Service. National Register of Historic Places Continuation Sheet, Section number 8, Page 26.
Santa Cruz Evening News, December 23, 1941.
United States Department of the Interior.

Roosevelt, Franklin, appeal to Hirohito
Salinas Morning Post, December 7, 1941.

SS *Luckenbach*, oil threat
California Department of Fish and Game, National Oceanic and Atmospheric Administration, U.S. Fish and Wildlife Service, National Park Service Report: S.S. Jacob Luckenbach and Associated Mystery Oil Spills November 1, 2006.

Union Oil, in regard to war damage trial
Civil Case #24101, National Archives, San Bruno Branch.
Lodi News-Sentinel, September 18, 1946.
Los Angeles Times, September 21, 1946.
Muncie Evening Press (Muncie, Indiana), September 12, 1946.
News-Pilot (San Pedro), September 14, 1946.
PBS.org "Brother Can You Spare Me a Billion? The story of Jesse H. Jones."*San Francisco Examiner*, September 12, 1946.

War Risk Insurance Demands
E. F. James December 24, 1941. Report of Casualty on the S. S. *Montebello*. Bureau of Customs.

Appendix

Montebello Crew List
December 23, 1941

Olof Ekstrom	Ernest Ross
John Young	William Shwederski
Kenneth McLean	Charles Richardson
William Barnhart	Edward Blunt
John Smith	John Silva
Fred Sanders	Edgar Smith
John Rossell	Paul Lewis
William Frez	Robert Welsh
John McIsaac	Arthur Johnson
John O'Connell	Carleen Silvas
Arthur Skola	Gordon Thomas
Donald Kingsbury	Maurice Albertson
Clarence White	Willis Cossident
John Sloan	Juanito Lozano
Richard Quincy	Vicente Amacio
Ray Settles	Charles Windley
William Cardnell	Abdon DeGarcia
Daniel Seed	Curtis Dennison
Michael Manning	Lorenzo Ygos

Coast Guard Casualty Report: Page 1

Form 2692
TREASURY DEPARTMENT
U. S. Coast Guard
Ed. Mar. 1928

REPORT OF CASUALTY

[Under Act June 20, 1874]

Collection District No. **27**, Port of **Los Angeles, California**

[See Instructions on Back]

1. Date (hour of day, day of week, day of month, year) — 1. **Dec. 23, 1941   5:40 A.M.**
2. Nationality, rig, name of vessel, service — 2. **Am. s/s Tanker " MONTEBELLO "**
3. Gross tonnage — 3. **8272 gross tons**
4. Age — 4. **Built in 1921**
5. Port where registered — 5. **Los Angeles, Calif.**
6. Official number — 6. **221100**
7. Name and residence of master — 7. **Olof W. Eckstrom, 8316 3rd Ave., Inglewood, Calif.**
8. Name and residence of owner — 8. **Union Oil Company of California Union Oil Bldg., Los Angeles, Cal**
9. Port last sailed from prior to casualty and date of sailing — 9. **Port San Luis, Calif. Dec. 23,1941**
10. Where bound — 10. **Vancouver, BC, Canada.**
11. Number of passengers — 11. **None**
12. Number of crew, including master, mates, etc. — 12. **38**
13. Number of persons lost (give names under Remarks) — 13. **None**
14. Estimated value of vessel — 14. **$1,200,000.00**
15. Estimated value of cargo — 15. **$67,317.45**
16. Nature of cargo — 16. **Bulk Crude Oil**
17. Had vessel a deckload? — 17. **No**
18. Was she overladen? — 18. **No**
19. Weight of cargo — 19. **10,920 tons.**
20. Estimated loss or damage to vessel — 20. **Total loss**
21. Estimated loss or damage to cargo — 21. **Total Loss**
22. Amount of insurance on vessel — 22. **$1,000,000.00**
23. Amount of insurance on cargo — 23. **$80,000.00**
24. Exact locality of casualty — 24. **Lat. 35°35'30"N   121°16'30" W**
25. Nature of casualty (foundering, stranding, collision, etc.). In case of collision, give name and hailing port of colliding vessel, if possible — 25. **Due to enemy action. Torpedoed. Vessel sunk.**
26. Cause of the casualty — 26. **Due to enemy action. Torpedoed.**

* Estimated total amount of loss is desired, without regard to what may be covered by insurance or expense incurred in floating vessel, and should be expressed in figures.

Coast Guard Casualty Report: Page 2

REPORT OF CASUALTY—Continued

27. Condition of weather and sea *_____ 27. NE 4 Choppy N W Sea

Overcast & Drizzle   Visibility 4 to 5 miles

28. State in detail measures taken to avoid casualty_____ 28. When enemy submarine was

sighted, started in zig-zag course

29. By whom and to what extent assistance was rendered_____ 29. None

30. Remarks. (All particulars not included in the foregoing will be here stated.)   30. At approximately 5:30 A.M. I sighted what appeared to be an enemy submarine on our starboard quarter. At once radioed to navy that enemy submarine was in the vicinity. I also ordered all possible speed and steared a zig-zag course. at 5:40 A.M. a terrific concussion was felt caused by a torpedo hitting on starboard side in No.3 or 2 tank below water edge. A general alarm was sounded. I ordered the radio operator to send S.O.S. but was informed that radio sets were out of order. Boats were lowered into the water and all hands checked during this procedure. Several shots were fired by the enemy. At 6:30 A.M. the vessel commenced sinking rapidly and at 6:45 A.M. was fully submerged. These boats were landed at Estero Bay and my boat which was punctured by a shell had to land in the surf south of Cambria.

Olof W. Ekstrom

12-30-41 _____ 19____   † _____ Master.

* Whether calm, gentle breeze, strong breeze, moderate gale, strong gale, storm, or hurricane.
† The person making this report will sign his name as managing owner, agent, or master, as the case may be.

NOTE.—Casualty report shall be forwarded to the COLLECTOR OF CUSTOMS in whose district the vessel is registered.

INSTRUCTIONS

Loss of property involved in any accident sustained or caused by a vessel of the United States, amounting to less than $300, will not be regarded as material loss or damage, and reports of such casualties, unless involving the loss of life or serious injury to any person, will not be required, except in cases of stranding, reports of which are desirable to aid in determining and locating points of danger to navigation. Reports will, however, be required in all cases of the total loss of vessels, although the amount involved may be less than $300.

In cases of stranding, where the amount of damage or loss of property is less than $300, answers may be required only to interrogatories Nos. 1 to 10, and 24 to 29 of this form; and in cases of loss of life, or serious injury to persons where the amount of damage or loss to the vessel and cargo is less than $300, answers should be required only to interrogatories Nos. 1 to 13, and 24 to 29.

In cases of collision, reports will be required from both the colliding vessels where the damage or loss of property of the two together amounts to $300, notwithstanding one of the vessels may have suffered little or no loss.

U. S. GOVERNMENT PRINTING OFFICE   2—2410

Union Oil's Notification of Intent to File Lawsuit

FORM 400 5-40 500M
PRINTED IN U.S.A.

IN REPLY GIVE NO.

Union Oil Company of California
Los Angeles, California
May 18, 1942

Mr. Reese H. Taylor, President

Att'n Mr.

Dear Sir:

At B u i l d i n g
Answering { Date-
Letter } File-

Subject <u>SINKING OF S.S. "MONTEBELLO"</u>

     On December 23, 1941, about 5:40 A.M., our tanker the S.S. "MONTEBELLO", while enroute from Port San Luis to Vancouver, British Columbia, with a cargo of crude oil consigned to Union Oil Company of Canada, Ltd., was struck by a torpedo from an enemy submarine and shortly thereafter sank. The place of sinking was about four miles southwest of the Piedras Blanca Lighthouse and in plain sight of persons on the shore at Port San Luis.

     On January 8th I wrote to Mr. Fayette B. Dow asking that a claim be made to the Reconstruction Finance Corporation for compensation for the loss of the vessel, and in connection therewith sent him a tentative form of itemized claim in which all relevant facts regarding the ship and its cargo, including valuations, were set forth. On January 15th Mr. Dow wrote to Mr. Jesse H. Jones, making a claim for such compensation. Since then from time to time I have corresponded with Mr. Dow regarding the matter and when at a recent date it appeared that an amendment to the act providing RFC funds for the War Damage Corporation had made it possible for us to recover such compensation, assuming that the President should determine the place where the "MONTEBELLO" was sunk "to be under the dominion and control of the United States", I further urged, in a letter to Mr. Dow dated May 11, 1942, that action be taken towards having it determined that the place where the "MONTEBELLO" was sunk was under the dominion and control of the United States, so that we might prosecute our claim.

     I am enclosing herewith for reference, and for your further information as to details, documents and letters to which I have referred.

Very truly yours,

Jerry H. Powell
Assistant Counsel

JHP/F
Encs.

RECORDED
IN
Treasurer's Office
Under

Claim No. M-?S
Initials M.H.

50

EXHIBIT "B"   X

Excerpts of Testimony by Montebello Crewmen

Captain Olof Ekstrom
Deposition

Attorney Jerry Powell

Q. Will you state your name?
A. Olof W. Ekstrom
Q. Where do you reside, Mr. Ekstrom?
A. 8816 Third Avenue, Inglewood, California.
Q. What is your occupation?
A. Shipmaster.
Q. By whom are you employed?
A. Union Oil Company of California.
Q. How long have you been so employed by Union Oil Company of California?
A. Approximately since 1926.
Q. State briefly in what capacity you have been so employed?
A. I have been employed as quartermaster for two years, third mate, second mate, chief mate, and master.
Q. What was your nautical experience prior to your being employed by Union Oil Company of California?
A. Well, I served on Swedish school ships for two and a half years, approximately.
Q. At what time?
A. From 1909 to 1911, Navy school ships. I was employed on sailing ships, British ships, Swedish merchant ships. I had eighteen months in the Swedish Navy as boatswain's mate from 1915 to 1916. From that time on I have been employed on various vessels of American registry, and served with the Shipping Board during the last war; Los Angeles Steamship Company, Admiral Lines, Associated Oil Company, and Union Oil Company.
Q. For what period of time have you been employed on ships

in coastwise traffic on the Pacific Coast?

A. Well, off and on I have been employed in the coastwise trade for approximately ten years.

Q. Are you in a position to state approximately how many trips you have made from San Luis Obispo northerly to Monterey or beyond during that period?

A. Oh, I would say at least over 300, approximately. Over 300 trips.

Q. During that time were you employed as a member of the deck personnel on the ships on which you worked?

A. I was employed as quartermaster and deck officer.

Q. With reference particularly to the part of the coast between San Luis Obispo and the Piedras Blancas Lighthouse, will you state what familiarity you have with the prevailing currents on the coast?

A. Well, at times I made up current reports for the United States Government on that particular coast, and I made up some current charts that were sent into the Hydrographic Office.

Q. Will you state how much time you have spent as an officer of the *Montebello* on that ship prior to December 23, 1941?

A. Well, I served on the *Montebello* several times; approximately 18 months to two years altogether.

Q. In what capacity again on that ship?

A. As chief officer, second officer, and as master.

Q. Were you employed on the *Montebello* on December 23, 1941?

A. Yes.

Q. At midnight on December 23, 1941, where was that ship?

A. It was anchored in Port San Luis Obispo Bay.

Q. Will you state briefly and in your own language what happened on December 23, 1941, with respect to the *Montebello*?

A. Well, I received orders from the Navy Department to proceed to sea, and I departed from Port San Luis; departure was taken from the breakwater at approximately 1:30 AM.

Allan Charles:

Q. Abeam of the breakwater, did you say?
A. Abeam of the breakwater approximately 1:30 in the morning. Then approximately at 2:43 I rounded Pt. Buchon.

[Powell continued:]

Q. Pardon me, Captain. I just want to say that I don't mean that you should go into precise detail as to everything you did, but state just in a general way what you did and what happened to the *Montebello*.
A. Well, I proceeded, I was bound for Vancouver, British Columbia; I left Port San Luis at 1:30 in the morning. Then I proceeded towards—I laid a course off Pt. Buchon to pass Piedras Blancas Lighthouse approximately 1½ miles off. Then around approximately 4:20 in the morning I heard gunfire, saw gun flashes astern of me. I called down to the engine room to give all possible speed and to disregard all safety precautions for speed. Approximately at 5:20 in the morning we sighted a submarine on the surface coming up astern of us, and I again called down to the engine room to give more speed, and reported by radio that a submarine tried to attack, which was received by the Navy Department. I then commenced to zigzag towards shore. At approximately 5:40 I was hit by a torpedo—what I assumed was a torpedo—on the starboard side, forepart of the vessel. Due to the concussion by the torpedo the vessel swung around towards left. We then tried to get another message out by wire but the wireless was put out of commission. Then I sent a message down to the engine room to secure the fires in the engine room. Of course, during that time I was ringing the general alarm. All hands were up on deck. I told them to stand by with the boats out. About ten minutes afterward we were fired upon by the submarine, gunshots fired, six or seven shots. Three boats got away inside of

about twenty minutes, and I stayed with the ship, together with five other men, until she started to go down. Then we loaded No. 1 boat, the boat left and we went into the boat. I would say around 6:40, about 6:40, she was fully submerged. She disappeared, went down by the head first and the stern came up about 150 feet in the air. At 6:40 she was fully submerged at the time when the flagstaff disappeared.

Q. Captain, at the time you sighted the submarine, was the light in the Piedras Blancas Lighthouse on and operating?

A. It was operating.

Q. Were you able to see the outline of the shore?

A. Yes. Between the squalls I could see the outline of the shore, between the rain squalls and drizzle.

Q. During your work and experience as an officer on board ship, has it been a part of your duties to estimate distance when at sea?

A. Yes, sir.

Q. Has it been a part of your duty to estimate the speed of ships from the deck?

A. Yes.

Q. Has your experience in that connection been such that you are familiar with the current and the effect of the wind and current upon the direction of a ship proceeding in the water?

A. Yes.

Q. In your judgment, how far were you from the coast at the time you sighted the submarine, approximately?

A. Well, approximately, I would say about three miles off.

Q. In your judgment, approximately how far from the coast were you at the time your ship was struck by the torpedo?

A. I should say approximately three miles.

Q. Well, were you the same distance from the coast at the time the torpedo struck you that you were when you first sighted the submarine?

A. Well, the coast is a little bit out, points sticking out, and rocks sticking out from the coastline, and it comes in toward Cambria, more like a cut in the coast. When you get further up, close to Piedras Blancas, you get out to a point, what we call Pt. Piedras Blancas.

Q. I believe you stated when you sighted the submarine you were approximately three miles from shore.

A. Approximately.

Q. Did you state that you then zigzagged toward the shore?

A. I zigzagged toward the shore, yes.

Q. Had you made any progress toward the shore when you were struck by the torpedo?

A. I must have done some, yes.

Q. Will you estimate approximately how far you had gone toward the shore?

A. Well, having zigzagged, I can't tell exactly, because I don't remember, but I made three-quarters of a mile or so toward shore.

Q. When you are speaking of the distance from the shore, are you speaking of what are known as statute miles as distinguished from nautical miles?

A. We always use nautical miles.

Q. I am speaking now of the distance from the shore.

A. Yes; the distance from the shore is always figured in nautical miles.

Q. Then am I to understand that when you sighted the submarine you were approximately three miles from the shore?

A. Approximately three miles.

Q. You had progressed toward the shore approximately three-quarters of a mile?

A. Yes; I figured I was approximately zigzagging toward shore about three-quarters of a mile.

Q. Than when you sighted the submarine?

A. Yes.

Q. What was the direction of the wind at that time?

A. Between north and northwest, I should say, magnetic. I went by magnetic, not true.

Q. What was the force of the wind?

A. I say about Force 4.

Q. Translated into layman's terms, how many miles an hour is that?

A. Say about fifteen to twenty miles per hour.

Q. Do you recall in what direction the bow of the boat was pointing at the time she sank?

A. When she sank she was pointed towards—in a southwesterly direction; I would say it would be about south or southwesterly direction after she turned around. She got hit and she turned around.

[Cross Examination.]

Mr. Charles: Q. Did you have a chance to save any of your logbooks or did all the ship's logs go down with the vessel?

A. All the ship's logs went down with the vessel.

Q. That, I suppose, would apply to the deviation book?

A. Everything went down, everything. My own property and the ship's property and all went down. I tried to open the safe in the dark, all lights went out, of course, when I was torpedoed. I tried to open the safe but I had to give it up, because I cannot open it with the combination like that by lighting a match. I lost my flashlight; in the explosion I was thrown onto the deck and I lost my flashlight.

Q. You did not have any small notebook or anything in your pocket that you made any notations in, I suppose? Was the chief officer in charge of the watch?

A. Yes.

Q. Do you know whether he made any entries in the log as you went up the coast from San Luis?

A. We did as far as it was possible to do so without exposing it too much light.

Q. Do you know whether he made those notations directly in

the rough log, or whether he made them on a scrap of paper, or in a notebook?

A. He might have done both of it.

Q. You don't know whether he saved the scraps of paper or the notebook?

A. No, I don't.

Q. As far as you know, there are not any records from the ship, itself, that were saved?

A. There is no record, whatsoever.

Q. Was the time, 1:30, your time of departure, your best recollection of the approximate time, or is that exact?

A. No; that is my closest recollection, and from other ships, too, when I left. I know my time was 1:30. The man from the dock in Port San Luis, he usually takes the time when we departed.

Q. You checked up with him afterward?

A. Yes.

Q. And he gave it to you?

A. My time, I remember it was 1:30, around that time, when I departed.

Q. What dock does the Union Oil use there; is that the middle dock?

A. Well, that is the only dock there is now—in Port San Luis, you mean?

Q. Yes.

A. Yes, that is a wharf [pointing to a display chart] that was put there that some railroads may run to, and that is the middle dock, yes. Well, Port San Luis Wharf is the north end. Then comes the Union Oil Company Wharf, and then the County Wharf, what they call it, a small wharf. There is only one place where big ships call.

Q. When you load do you load at the dock, or are you out at loading buoys—

A. No. We load at the dock tied up to the dock and to the buoy.

[Further in his cross-examination, Mr. Charles's questioning shifted to the reported zigzag maneuvering.]

Q. Which wing [of the bridge] were you on after the submarine was sighted?

A. Well, I was on both sides, off and on, on one side and then the other.

Q. Let's go back to the point where you gave the order that you believe was hard right first. Now, about how long did you have the helmsman hold the hard right rudder before you gave him another order?

A. Well, maybe two or three minutes; less than that.

Q. Well now—

A. I will say less than two minutes.

Q. I know it is difficult to ask you to remember all the details under the excitement that existed at the time, but I was wondering if you could recall whether you had formulated any plan in your mind about that zigzagging; did you intend to hold to that right rudder long enough to get your stern off the original course, or did you have in mind swinging back in the other direction before your stern had a chance to get off the original course?

A. Well, of course, the stern, when I say "Hard right" and go full speed the ship will start swinging.

Q. She would start swinging right away?

A. Slowly, and then increase speed as she goes in.

Q. But it would take two or three minutes before her stern would get off that original course, even at full speed, wouldn't it?

A. No, I wouldn't say—off her regular course, I wouldn't say that long, because the whole ship swings together.

Q. Yes, but she would go four or five ship lengths, wouldn't she, Captain, before the stern would really get off that original course to the right? Do you see what I mean?

A. Yes, but if you look at the wake of a ship when it swings, the minute she starts swinging the wake will have a curve in it; the stern will swing at the same time. Of course, she won't swing so fast, but the stern will swing from the moment you turn the wheel hard over.

Q. But to get your stern over to the right of your original course will take a couple of minutes, won't it, under those conditions?

A. I don't understand what you mean.

Q. Let me explain this: If you want to turn as fast as you can to the right—

A. Yes.

Q. You give your helmsman a hard right rudder order, don't you?

A. Yes.

Q. The first thing that happens is that your stern moves off a little bit to the left as your bow moves to the right?

A. Yes.

Q. Your bow keeps swinging to the right?

A. Yes.

Q. About how far would your ship go forward in the water before the stern, which has moved a little to the left of your course, gets over the right angle and starts to pull away from that original course?

A. A stern would swing at the same moment as the bow swings.

Q. Yes, that is true, but how long does it take before that gets off the line of your original course?

A. That is something I never figured out.

Q. Well, let me ask you another question or two, to be sure I understand the situation. She is a single screw?

A. Yes, a single screw.

Q. Is it a turbine?

A. Steam reciprocating engine.

Q. Right hand screw?

A. A right hand propeller.

Q. Going back, I will ask you the question as to what order you gave, first of all, after sighting the submarine, to the helmsman. I understood you to say you are not sure, but you think it was "Right rudder"?

A. I am not positively sure, but sometimes when you say,

"Right," like that, he says, "Hard right."

Q. You think you held that for two or three minutes?

A. Well, I know we held it a very short time.

Q. Might have been less than two or three minutes?

A. Yes.

Q. Do you recall, then, the order you gave after that?

A. Then, "Hard left."

Q. You are sure it was "Hard left", not just "20 degrees left," or "30 degrees left"?

A. Well, in swinging, in order to get the fast swinging you give him "Hard over," in order to get a quick swing of a ship. Then when she starts swinging you tell him, "Ease her; ease the helm," and to stop a quick swing to steady her up.

Q. Your best recollection is after you held her hard right about two minutes or less you then gave the order, "Hard left"?

A. Yes.

Q. Have you any recollection about how long you held that hard left rudder?

A. Well, it was only a very, very short time.

Q. About the same?

A. In order to stop from swinging you change to the right, give the order to stop the left swinging and to the right.

Q. Yes. Then do you recall whether you got another rudder order in before you got the torpedo?

A. Yes, I had several.

Q. Several more?

A. In ten minutes' time I had several maneuvers in there to the rudder.

Q. Do you recall whether or not you alternated more or less to the right or to the left?

A. I alternated more to the right.

Q. More rudder orders to the right than to the left?

A. Yes. I wanted to get in closer to the coast in case I get sunk.

Q. But you did not hold her on a right rudder for a long time? I mean you did not make any right angle turn, or anything like that?

A. No. I would turn clear around that way.

Q. Did the submarine stay behind you all the time until you were attacked, or did she come up abeam of you, or on your quarter at any time?

A. Well, at that time I was more interested to get away from the submarine, and I had two men to keep a lookout on the submarine and inform me where the submarine was located.

Q. Who were those men?

A. The chief officer, McLean, is his name, and, I believe, a sailor named, Frez.

Q. Where did you place them?

A. I had them astern of the vessel; they could see better from there.

Q. When did you send them astern?

A. As soon as I sighted the submarine.

Q. Had you been out on the bridge all the time from Port San Luis, or had you gone into the chart room to lie down at any time before the submarine was reported?

A. No. I was on the bridge except I went in the chart room to check the course by the light.

Q. Who first sighted the submarine, do you know?

A. I don't remember. I believe it was the chief officer, McLean.

Q. The ten minutes that you estimated elapsed from the time the submarine was first sighted until the ship was torpedoed, was that based upon your best estimate of the amount of time that was involved, or how did you figure that, Captain?

A. When I first sighted the submarine, I sent in a message to the Navy Department that a submarine tried to attack, and I cannot say it was exactly ten minutes; it might have been more, might have been less. The only thing I know, it was a long ten minutes.

Q. You mean from the time you sent the message until she was torpedoed?

A. Yes.

Q. Then the ten minutes you have just estimated to the best of your ability?

A. Yes.

Q. Based upon your knowledge of the approximate time when you sent that S.O.S.?

A. Yes.

Q. I wonder if you would again tell us, so we will be sure we have all the steps in mind, what you did as soon as the submarine was sighted, all the things you did. You sent the radio message first, did you?

A. Sent the radio message.

Q. Where was the radio operator?

A. He was in the radio room.

Q. You sent somebody in?

A. No. I told him—

Q. Personally?

A. No. I told him by speaking tube.

Q. Do you recall just what you told him?

A. Yes. I also sent the second office, Mr. Young, I sent him down to the radio room to be sure he got the message off.

Q. Did the radio operator read back to you the message that he was going to send?

A. He did report it back, yes.

Q. Do you recall what the message said?

A. I recall, "Submarine trying to attack." I sent out an S.O.S. at the time. Sent "S.O.S. Submarine trying to attack." That is all I sent in, and the position, of course.

Q. Do you recall what position you gave?

A. I believe I gave four miles southwesterly of Piedras Blancas.

Q. Did you have to stop and chart that before you gave the message, or did you already know just what the position was?

A. That was taken approximately.

Q. About how far off do you think that was likely to have been from exact, Captain?

A. I figured at the time I was exactly at the place.

Q. That was the only position you gave in that radio message, wasn't it?

A. That was the only position I gave.

Q. Then what other things did you do; you gave an extra jingle on the telegraph for speed?

A. I gave—I told them to give every possible speed they could get and disregard all safety precautions.

Q. You did that then by the speaking tube?

A. By telephone.

Q. You did not use the telegraph?

A. No; I was on the telephone.

Q. You wouldn't be sure?

A. I probably gave them a jingle on the telegraph; I don't recall that, but I probably did.

Q. Which did you do first, do you recall, arrange for the radio message or give the extra speed?

A. I arranged for the radio message first.

Q. Then you called for extra speed?

A. Yes.

Q. Then you started zigzagging?

A. Then I started zigzagging.

Q. You did not start zigzagging before you did those other things?

A. No, I probably didn't.

Q. At that time, almost immediately you sent these men back on the poop to watch the submarine, did you?

A. Yes.

Q. Did they give you a report from time to time as to the position?

A. They gave me reports, yes, that the submarine was getting closer.

Q. How did they do that? Have you got a telephone?

A. Well, this sailor was along. He was a messenger running between the chief officer back and forth.

Q. You did not use a telephone there, you say?

A. No. There was a telephone, but it was up on top, back aft, and not used then.

Q. The submarine stayed right behind you all the time?

A. He stayed behind me, keeping on getting closer and closer.

Q. At the time the submarine was first sighted by you, about how far astern of you was it?

A. Oh, probably there was a mile or so.

Q. Could you see a mile in that weather?

A. You could see a mile, all right.

Q. In darkness?

A. Yes. You could see a mile regardless of rain. You could see a mile, or three-quarters of a mile. You could see that. It was not too muggy.

Q. What could you see, just a light on the submarine, or did you see the silhouette?

A. Saw the silhouette of it.

Q. You could see it was a submarine?

A. Yes; there was no question about that.

Q. It was all the way out of the water, then?

A. Yes, all the way out.

Q. Whom did you have on the bridge with you besides the chief officer and Frez, anybody?

A. Yes; the second officer, Mr. Young, and also a seaman by the name of Quincy.

Q. Do you recall hearing any fog signals at any time before the ship was torpedoed?

A. No; no fog signals.

Q. Do you recall hearing any after she was torpedoed?

A. No.

Q. How was your wheelhouse clock, was that correct?

A. Yes, fairly correct.

Q. Do you recall having taken any notations from the time that you left the breakwater until the S.O.S. call was given, do you recall any times in between?

A. Well, all kinds of notes were made and were written down in the log book by the officer on watch.

Q. Yes, I understand that. But you don't know yourself?

A. No. That is done—that is the officer's duty to do that without being told by the master.

Q. What was the full speed of the Montebello under ordinary conditions, Captain?

A. Well, loaded, her speed was ten knots loaded.

Q. About how many revolutions would that be?

A. Say about sixty-four; between sixty-four and sixty-six.

Q. You were going about that speed, were you, through the water prior to the time when you called for the extra speed?

A. Well, I called for the extra speed about an hour before I sighted the submarine.

Q. That was before you had gotten a report that there were enemy submarines in the vicinity?

A. I don't have that report. I have that report later, but he was shooting, gunfire behind me.

Q. You saw the gunfire behind you?

A. Yes. Then afterward I got the message to stay clear of the area.

Q. Had you done any zigzagging at all prior to the time when the submarine was reported?

A. No.

Q. Do you recall, Captain, just how your rudder was turned at the time the torpedo struck the ship?

A. No, I don't recall.

Q. It struck about where, the torpedo?

A. Struck in the starboard side up forward, between either No. 1 or No. 2 tank, maybe.

Q. Did you give any rudder order after the torpedo struck?

A. No. The rudder was out of commission.

Q. Immediately?

A. Immediately.

Q. Were the engines stopped immediately?

A. Well, the engine was stopped shortly after.

Q. What did you do, did you hail the engine room on the speaking tube?

A. I sent verbal orders down to secure everything in the engine room.

Q. By that you mean put the fires out in the boilers?

A. Yes.

Q. Stop the engines?

A. Yes.

Q. About how long after the striking did you do that, a matter of seconds, or a minute or two?

A. A matter of minutes.

1st Asst. Engineer William Seed Courtroom Testimony

Attorney Edward Ransom

Q. What boat did you leave [the *Montebello*] in, if any?

A. As we passed this No. 4 boat we could hear them down there shouting and swearing, trying to get their falls released, and so I grabbed the forward fall on it and went right down it, and the mate grabbed the after fall and went down the after fall. That is how we came to be in No. 4 lifeboat.

Q. Did you make any observations at that time as to whether the *Montebello* was moving through the water?

A. She was not moving through the water.

Q. At that time did you make any observation to determine which way the shore was?

A. Yes, I did.

Q. Could you see the shoreline by then?

A. Not right then, no. We had to pull around the end of the ship before we could see the shoreline. At that time the ship was between us and the shore.

Q. Before getting into the lifeboat were you able to see anything to indicate to you in which direction the shore was?

A. We were on the offshore side looking out to sea.

Q. Could you see any mountains in the background?

A. There wasn't—the ship was heading northwest and we were facing the western side.

Q. That is when you were in the lifeboat?

A. Yes.

Q. How did you leave the ship then, what direction did the lifeboat go?

A. We rowed around to our left and went under the stern of the ship, heading to shore.

Q. How many were rowing?

A. At no time was there more than four of us rowing and sometimes only three.

Q. As you rowed away, were you able to see the *Montebello*?

A. Yes.

Q. Did you see the *Montebello* sink?

A. I did.

Q. Do you know about what time she sank?

A. Approximately ten minutes to seven.

Q. How do you know that?

A. By my wrist watch.

Q. You looked at your watch?

A. I did.

Q. Was it dark at that time?

A. It was getting light by that time.

Q. What could you see of the *Montebello* when she sank?

A. You could see the whole ship; she went down slowly by the bow.

Q. You could see it clearly?

A. I could see her very clearly.

Q. By that time could you see the shoreline?

A. Yes; I saw the mountains, which is the shoreline, the mountains come right directly up to it.

Q. Do you know what direction the *Montebello* was heading?

A. In a general northwesterly direction.

Q. Could you see the breakers at any time?

A. No, we could not.

Q. In your approximately twenty years at sea up to that time, what experience had you had in measuring distances?

A. Well, the same as anybody else that is looking for the shoreline and figuring what time he is going to get home, being on the deck when you approach the land.

Q. Did you form any estimate of the distance your small boat was from the *Montebello* at the time the *Montebello* sank?

A. Yes, I did.

Q. What would you estimate that distance to be?

A. Between one and one-half and two miles.

Q. The small boat was between the *Montebello* and the shore, is that your testimony?

A. That's right.

Q. Did you form any estimate at the time the *Montebello* sank of the distance from your lifeboat to the land?

A. Yes, I did.

Q. What was the distance?

A. Between three and one-half and four miles; maybe a little over.

Q. Having estimated the distance between your boat and the *Montebello,* and your boat and the shore, what did you estimate the distance the *Montebello* was from the shore at the time she sank?

A. Five miles, maybe a little over; between five and six, I would say.

Q. Was there any wind at that time?

A. I don't exactly recall; not what you would call a strong wind, no.

Q. Could you determine if your boat drifted in any current at all, your lifeboat?

A. Well, it is hard to tell when you are drifting in a small boat, all you can do is pull for the shore.

Q. So the answer is that you don't know?

A. I don't know.

Q. Do you know what time it was when you left the *Montebello?*

A. Yes.

Q. What time would you say?

A. It was about quarter past six.

Q. Did you row all the way to shore?

A. No. We used a sail part way.

Q. How much of the time did you use a sail?

A. I would say not over fifteen minutes at the most.

Q. Did you ultimately land with your boat, or were you picked up on the way?

A. We were picked up.

Q. About how far offshore would you say you were picked up?

A. Maybe around a half-mile.

Q. Do you have any idea what time it was when you were picked up?

A. Oh, as near as I can estimate now, it was around quarter to eight.

Q. Could you estimate the speed of your rowboat?

A. No.

Mr. Sandmeyer: He is not qualified to do that. There is no showing he is, at least.

Mr. Ransom: His answer is "No."

Radio Operator William Barnhart Deposition

Attorney William Brainerd

Q. Mr. Barnhart, you understand that you are under oath, and that you are to tell the truth?

A. Yes, sir.

Q. Calling your attention to December 23, 1941, at that time were you employed on board the Steamship *Montebello*?

A. I was.

Q. In what capacity?

A. Radio operator.

Q. How long had you been employed as radio operator on that vessel?

A. Since December 4.

Q. Was that at the beginning of the voyage?

A. That was the beginning of my employment aboard the vessel.

Q. Where did you sign on, do you recall?

A. Port San Luis

Q. Was this the first run of the vessel from Port San Luis—

A. No, it was not.

Q. Let me finish the question—since you signed on?

A. No. We sailed to Vancouver, British Columbia, and returned, and were starting a new voyage.

Q. On this new voyage, do you recall the time that the ship left Port San Luis?

A. Well, as I recall, it was in the vicinity of 1:00 to 2:00 o'clock. I don't recall exactly the time.

Q. Do you happen to recall approximately the time that the ship was attacked?

A. I know the exact time we were torpedoed, because I was sending a message. It was 5:47 AM.

Q. From the time that you left Port San Luis at 1:00 or 2:00 o'clock until the time that you were torpedoed, what were your duties?

A. Well, my legal duties were to maintain one hour's watch after leaving port. I maintained that watch, and a little more. At approximately 3:00 o'clock, somewhere around that time, I don't remember the exact time, I got a message from a ship, that sent a war call, and I wasn't able to determine what the name of the ship was. It was attacked approximately abeam of us, or possibly behind us. That was the only message that I received of any consequence.

Q. In other words, your duties then were as a radio operator; is that correct?

A. That is correct.

Q. Were you on watch continuously from the time the ship left Port San Luis until you were torpedoed?

A. No.

Q. How much of the time were you off watch during that time?

A. Oh, I would say not more than half an hour.

Q. Do you recall about what time that half an hour interval took place?

A. Yes. Shortly after 3:00 o'clock I went off watch—well, let's see; shortly before 3:00 o'clock I went off watch, and shortly after 3:00 I was called on watch, at the time that they thought they heard gunfire, and I stood a watch then again for about an hour, and then went off watch again for just a few minutes, and then I was called back on watch again.

Q. In all you say you missed about half an hour?

A. I believe that would be pretty close.

Q. Who else would be at the radio during that half an hour?

A. No one; auto alarm.

Q. What do you mean?

A. That is an automatic signaling device that you have to send a certain signal with, when you are in distress, and it rings a bell, usually, and in the case of extreme emergency they don't have time, or they wouldn't have time to send a signal to acknowledge it.

Q. Would that catch incoming messages as well as outgoing?

A. No, it doesn't catch any incoming messages at all. It only rings a bell, if you have time to send the warning signal.

Q. Now, during the time that you were on watch, did you receive any radio messages other than the one you have just described of the ship being attacked?

A. The messages that I received, specifically the only one that would have any bearing on this case, would be the message that I received from the S.S. *Larry Doheny*. They sent a message, as near as I can remember, they said, "Attacked by enemy raider three miles off Estero Bay." They sent a war call, and that I wasn't able to determine their identity; and then I heard another message too that was amplified.

Q. What time was that, do you know?

A. That was somewhere around 3 AM. I can't make it any more

definite than that.

Q. Did you receive any other messages?

A. I don't recall any others in particular. It is just the normal flow of traffic. I wouldn't remember. It was none of any consequence.

Q. Do you recall any message pertaining to routing of the ship?

A. No. I have since found out that they sent us a message diverting our routing; three hours later, after we were sunk.

Q. From whom?

A. This is merely something that I found out from other radio operators. It was sent to us from the Navy station at San Francisco.

Q. During the time you were on watch, you received no such message?

A. No such message, no, sir.

Q. Do you recall what messages you sent during the time, or from the time you left Port San Luis until the time you were struck by a torpedo?

A. Well, I don't recall.

Q. If any?

A. I don't recall whether I sent a departure notice or not.

Q. Did you send any others?

A. I don't recall whether we did. We might have sent a departure notice, which would be encoded.

Q. What was the first message you sent out pertaining to the attack?

A. I sent a message that the captain ordered. He gave me the message over the speaking tube to send this: "Sighted submarine four and a half miles off Piedras Blancas light."

Q. Was that all the message?

A. That is what he ordered me to send.

Q. Was that coupled with an S.O.S.?

A. No. I addressed it to all U.S. ships, and I was answered by N.P.G., San Francisco; a Naval radio station.

Q. In which direction was your ship headed at the time?

A. Towards Canada; north.

Q. North?

A. Yes; northwest, approximately.

Q. Do you know of your own knowledge whether that submarine would be to your port or to your starboard of the ship as it headed north?

A. At what time?

Q. At the time you were given that message to send.

A. Well, as far as I know, they were on the starboard side, inshore of us.

Q. Did you send any other messages pertaining to the torpedoing?

A. No.

Q. Didn't you, if I may ask that leading question?

A. No; because the first warning I had of any submarine attack at all was the message that the captain gave me, and before I got that completely sent we were torpedoed.

Q. I take it that the radio was struck, was it?

A. No. It struck below the radio room, and the equipment was rendered inoperative as a result of the torpedoing.

Q. Do you recall receiving a message by radio from the Navy, stating that the *Larry Doheny* had been fired upon by the enemy, and ordering all boats to clear that area? Do you recall that message received?

A. No, I do not recall any such message. I recall only the message that the *Larry Doheny* itself sent, which stated that they were being fired upon by an enemy raider.

Q. You don't recall receiving a message from the Navy?

A. No. I definitely do not recall any such message.

Q. Now, if the captain testifies under oath that he received such a message through you, or through the radio room, you wouldn't dispute that testimony, would you?

A. Well, I can only say that in this manner, that it has been 5-years, and I recall no such message. However, if I delivered any such message to him, it could be very easily, but I don't recall it. I would have delivered it to him if I had received any such message, but I don't recall it.

Q. Now, this message that the captain ordered you to send that the submarine was sighted, you do not recall the time when the submarine was sighted by the officer on deck? You wouldn't know that?

A. Well, it would be a very few minutes before I was ordered to send a message, because that would be the first thing they would do; order a message sent.

Q. That may be a conclusion.

A. No, I don't know the exact time. I only know the time I was ordered to send the message.

Q. You do not now recall after these four or five years the exact words of that message?

A. That I was ordered to send?

Q. Yes.

A. I have already quoted them here.

Q. Now, that message had been picked up, and we have a record of it.

A. Yes.

Q. Wasn't the message: "Sighted submarine about four miles off Piedras Blancas?"

A. That is in substance the message, yes.

Q. Now, the submarine was actually sighted first on the port quarter. You didn't know about that?

A. Yes, I know about that, because it was sighted at sea from us.

Q. Now, when you were at what you considered the nearest point of land, what was that point?

A. Well, I thought it was Piedras Blancas because of the fact that the message was given me, and I know we had very little time to get past it, and I would consider that the nearest point of land, Piedras Blancas.

Q. When you say that you saw this point of land, that is the point you are talking about?

A. That is correct, where the lighthouse was.

Q. Where were you when you saw this point?

A. Immediately after coming out of the radio room; after the torpedoing.

Q. Everything was pretty excited about that time, wasn't it?

A. Naturally, it would be.

Q. Everybody is trying to find themselves a lifeboat, and you were being shelled by the submarine, weren't you?

A. That is correct.

Q. At that time it was till dark?

A. Yes.

Q. It was overcast overhead?

A. I couldn't make any positive statement as to that.

Q. You don't recall whether it was or not?

A. No.

Q. Actually, it was drizzling too, wasn't it?

A. I don't recall any drizzle.

Q. Was there any wind?

A. Very little wind at that time, I believe. It blew up later. At that time I don't think there was much wind.

Q. Now, in the dark you just saw the light, is that right?

A. I could see Point Piedras Blancas, a very vague shoreline.

Q. Even in the dark?

A. It was a good ways away, but you could make it out.

[Later in his testimony, Barnhart was asked where his lifeboat had been picked up by the tug Alma. He responded his boat was rescued, he thought, past the point at Piedras Blancas. This was in conflict with the testimony from survivors of other lifeboats.]

Q. You don't mean that you were picked up north of this light?

A. That is correct.

Q. Is that true?

A. Precisely.

Q. It was a Standard Oil launch that picked you up?

A. A Standard Oil tug.

Q. If those people show that they picked up your boat near Cayucos, which I believe is south of Piedras Blancas, what would you say about that?

A. I know where we were picked up, and I know we had a good long trip before we got to Cayucos.

Q. Weren't you picked up between Cambria and Cayucos?

A. As I say, I don't know the towns up there. I only know in relation to this particular point, and that is all the information I can give you; just the information in relation to that one point.

Lightkeeper Norman Francis
Courtroom Testimony

Attorney Allan Charles

Q. Mr. Francis, what is your occupation?

A. I am Officer in Charge of a light station, an enlisted man in the Coast Guard, Boatswain's Mate, Coast Guard.

Q. At what lighthouse are you now stationed?

A. Piedras Blancas Light Station near San Simeon, California.

Q. About how long have you been there?

A. About twelve and a half years.

Q. Have you been there twelve and a half years continuously?

A. Continuously, yes, sir.

Q. Were you at the station on December 22 and December 23, 1941?

A. I was, sir.

Q. Could you tell us what your duties are at the station, or, rather, what your duties were at the station on December 22 and 23, 1941?

A. My duties at the station are varied, as Officer in Charge, to see to the maintenance of the station, maintenance of the operational equipment, aides to navigation, and the maintenance of the watches and duties stood by my assistants, general observation of all in the vicinity, like shipping, and so forth, weather conditions, and also taking weather observations for the airways.

Q. Were you taking any such observations during the year 1941?

A. Yes, sir.

Q. And during December?

A. Yes, sir.

Q. Were you on duty at any time on the early morning of December 23, 1941?

A. I was on duty at 0400, 4 o'clock in the morning, until 8 o'clock.

Q. Did you receive any reports of any difficulties of any kind early that morning?

A. I had reports early in the evening that there was submarine action going on off Estero Bay and Point Buchon.

Q. Did you receive any further reports?

A. Later in the morning—I think it was a little after 0400 in the morning I received a report which at that time came through Cayucos, the army base, Standard Oil, Estero Bay, that submarine action was going on near the vicinity of the station and that there was a ship involved.

Q. Did you yourself observe anything unusual on that morning?

A. Not until I got that report.

Q. When you got that report what did you do?

A. We set an observation—there were six men at the station on duty at the time with myself and we set an observation to see if we could identify any action going on.

Q. From where did you observe?

A. We had our point of observation at the base of the light tower. We were standing watch in the open. We had no lookout building at that time, so we were standing—there was a soldier at the top of the tower, a soldier at the base, and I had two seamen and my first-assistant, the keeper and myself were standing at the base of the tower at the time. Each man was given a direction or position to stand from which to observe around the vicinity of the station at that point.

Q. Would you go on and tell the jury in your own words what, if anything, you observed?

Mr. Sandmeyer: This is limited to what he himself, the witness, observed.

Mr. Charles: I believe that is what I said or meant to say—what you observed.

A. At the time I was standing at the base of the tower facing in a southerly direction.

Q. Could I ask you about what time that was?

A. That was about 5:30, as I remember it, when I observed a gun flashing. At that time the visibility was quite obscured by moderate rain, so that visibility at that time probably was only about a half a mile, possibly less ordinarily. However, this gun flash that I saw flashed out in the rain, and about the time that I saw it two or three other men with me at the time observed it also. We stood looking in that direction, and we observed two more flashes, gunfire. That was all, though. There wasn't anything else visible but the gun flashes.

At that time I unconsciously made a note of the direction, and I estimated in discussing with the men just about how far out these gun flashes were—we thought it was about five miles. That was just guessing due to the reduced visibility caused by the rain. We couldn't hear the explosions of the gun, as at that time the wind was blowing quite brisk from the northwest, so that it would have carried the sound of gunfire away from the station.

Q. Was the lighthouse light on all this time?

A. Yes, sir, the light was on, and the fog signal was in operation.

Q. How long did the fog signal continue to operate that day?

A. The fog signal was started about 4:30 and discontinued operation about 5:55. The gun flashes took place during that time, around 5:30, but it occurred during that period of obscured visibility.

Q. Would you describe what type of gun flashes they were? Were they long flashes, were they short flashes, or what type of flashes were they?

A. As I remember it, the flashes were rather short, but distinct in a flare like, but heavy—but they had a tendency—well, the way it looked to me, it looked like the flashes were firing shoreward, as I noted at the time, and as I can remember it now.

Q. Do you remember about how many flashes you heard?

A. Three. I didn't hear them.

Q. I mean you saw them?

A. I saw three flashes.

Q. Did you hear any firing?

A. No sound at all, no, sir.

Q. I wonder if you would, so the matter may be clear to the jury, describe what type of land your lighthouse is located on and how high the lighthouse is?

A. The lighthouse is located on a point of land projecting out from the mainland possibly a quarter of a mile. The height of the tower, the base of the tower, that point at which we were standing, was sixty or seventy feet above sea level. This point of land—it is like a peninsula. It is not an island. It is part of the mainland.

Q. Had you any experience in any of the wars in observing gun flashes or gunfire?

A. In World War I, when I was in the army, I had field piece practice at night under rainy conditions, hazy conditions.

Q. In your work do you have any occasion to make observations and estimates of distances?

A. Well, I have had in the past. I used to be stationed at the light station at San Pedro. I had been there six years. And part of our work was to observe the movements of vessels, positions, and so forth, at different times. And certain instances have occurred where we have been asked to give positions of vessels at a time—certainly collisions, and so forth—and distances, and other different weather conditions. Points that probably I was not conscious of at the time I subconsciously registered and was able to give information on when questioned at a later date.

Q. Did you have any occasion to observe the passage of ships beyond your point during the war time?

A. Yes, we observed movements of quite a number of vessels.

Q. Do you have any rocks around the end of the point on which the lighthouse is located?

A. Yes, there are some rocks, but they do not extend very far out from the point.

Q. About how far from the point is the farthest rock?

A. I would say approximately three hundred yards. They will project above the water at low tide.

Q. I wonder if you could tell us how close you have seen vessels pass the point during war time at night?

A. At night? Well, observation at night is somewhat different from the day—however, certain types of vessels come in pretty close—I would say a quarter of a mile at the closest. Perhaps we can see that by night observation and the running lights of the ship.

Q. How far off do you see them sometimes?

A. On the horizon, which is approximately nine miles from that elevation of this light, and they vary anywhere from a quarter of a mile to six or seven miles offshore from the life station.

Q. In that connection, have you made any observation as to how far from the point you have seen tankers come?

A. I have seen that they range anywhere from possibly two miles to six or seven miles off the light, generally. That is, oil tankers proceeding in and out from Estero Bay.

Q. Could you arrive at any judgment as to the approximate place off the coast the flashes of light occurred, flashes of gunfire occurred?

A. Well, at the position I was standing at the time, I would say approximately five miles from the station in a south, southeast direction, and the nearest point to the station there is San Simeon, which projects further out than the point; between the station and San Simeon I would say, possibly.

Q. In what direction from the station was that?

A. As near as I could determine I would say south, southeast.

Q. Do you recall, Mr. Francis, an engineer by the name of Parker Palmer calling upon you with a transit about a year ago?

A. Yes.

Q. Did you at that time make any effort to show him the direction in which you had seen the gun flashes?

A. Yes, I had. They asked me and I helped them, and I gave the position as I remembered standing at that time at the base of the tower, and the direction which I was facing, and the transit was set up, and I think Mr. Bartholomew, Mr. Palmer, and Mr. Bartholomew, I directed him—before I go further, there was a rock sticking out twenty or thirty feet high above the bluff below the light in that direction which I was facing, and I used that as a point; it happened to impress me at that time and I noted that on that morning at a later date when I was asked about it, and being familiar with all the contour of the station that sort of registered, that rock at the time, so I used that as the point at which I was standing in determining the direction in which I saw the gun flashes. I sighted them on the transit and Mr. Bartholomew was down below there and walked across in front of that rock until I directed him to the position in which I lined it up for his bearing, and they took the bearing on that point.

Q. Had you observed the gun fire with relation to that rock?

A. Well, at the time I hadn't, but I subconsciously sort of later on made up my mind that that rock was in line, and I sort of subconsciously noted that.

Mr. Charles: I think that is all.

[Cross Examination.]

Mr. Sandmeyer: Q. Mr. Francis, your last testimony was that four and one-half years ago when you were looking at those flashes you did not line the flashes up with any particular point; that is correct, isn't it.

A. At the time I observed the gun flashes?

Q. Yes, back in 1941.

A. No; at that time, no, I hadn't taken any particular point of them concerning the rock.

Q. Weren't you at that time trying to fix the exact course or bearing that those flashes were from?

A. No.

Q. It was only later that you recalled you had seen the lights out in that direction and sort of lined up the flashes being somewhere along where that rock was; is that correct?

A. That came into my mind that I had observed the rock, like I explained, subconsciously; my experience in determining distance or point of observation for taking bearings and so forth, my work naturally covers a lot of that, and you unconsciously note a lot of details that might not come to your mind at that time but later on they came to my mind.

Q. You saw the flashes from what you testified was in a south, southeast direction; is that correct?

A. That is the position I gave you.

Q. You recall after two or three years that you saw this rock out in a south, southeast direction?

A. Yes, that's right.

Q. But you would not attempt at this time, or even a year ago, to give the exact bearing that you saw the flashes, would you?

A. I remember that little point. I would have given it to—

Q. You mean just a general south, southeasterly direction?

A. Taking that rock as a bearing and where I was standing, judging without the aid of a compass, and I explained that it was that direction, south, southeasterly direction, using the rock and where I was standing as a sort of bearing.

Q. The point I am making is, you testified, both on direct and in answer to my question that at the time you saw the flashes you did not line them up with the rock?

A. Naturally I didn't at the time, because lots of times you don't pay attention to observations, but unconsciously those details register later on, so that is part of my work, to make observations, and probably I don't pay much attention at the time.

Q. When you say south, southeasterly, is that true or compass?

A. Well, now, I wouldn't know; like I say, that was my observation without the aid of a compass, magnetic.

Q. When you say it was at a south, southeasterly direction you would not get it down to such a narrow range as to say it was compass or true, would you?

A. No; that was my guess, and that is still my guess.

Q. You described it as such on your direct examination?

A. Yes.

Q. As being your guess.

A. That is all any of it was, as far as that goes.

Q. Didn't you say you thought the visibility was only about half a mile?

A. Yes, I would say visibility for observing a ship was approximately a half a mile, as far as that goes, but the light was revolving around and the light will at that close proximity swing around in that vicinity.

Q. If the visibility was one-half mile, anything that would be further away from the point than a half a mile you would not be expected to see, being blacked out?

A. You couldn't see under ordinary conditions as I assumed them at that time more than half a mile. It was raining.

Q. And there was a strong wind from the northwest, too, that would be blowing southeasterly from the point from where the lighthouse is?

A. Yes, the wind was blowing northwesterly at the time.

Q. That is, blowing in a southeasterly direction?

A. Well, naturally, from the north.

Q. Was that a pretty strong wind?

A. It was blowing pretty brisk; I believe it was blowing around, I would say at that time around thirty-two miles an hour.

Q. So that noise from the guns would be blown away from you?

A. You could not have heard anything due to the wind velocity.

Q. When you say you guessed them to be about five miles away, that is a pretty rough guess, too, isn't it?

A. No, not too exact. In giving condensed reports, and particularly during the war time on your observations, they are confined more or less strictly to distance and direction. If you made a report about any movement of a ship you had to give the direction and the distance as close as you could, so you naturally would study those two points stronger than possibly the rest of your report.

Q. Except that the war had been going on about two weeks?

A. Well, it was going on then.

Q. But you would not have had the experience—

A. I had some eighteen or twenty years experience observing all kinds of weather and conditions. Weather observation also, I have had considerable experience in that. In fact, I have been active in all of them much more than the average layman.

Q. No doubt about that. You did not see the submarine, did you?

A. No.

Q. If it were in the area that you thought it was could somebody down in Cambria have seen the submarine, do you think?

A. It is possible, if it was clear enough. I don't know whether they did, or not.

Q. It was pretty bad.

A. It was at the station, but it may have been clear at Cambria at the time. That is a weather phenomenon.

Q. But you don't know what it would be in between?

A. I don't know what was in between. I could only tell from my point of observation.

Q. All you saw were the flashes?

A. Yes.

Q. You were of the opinion that they were, or the flashes you saw were from gun shooting shoreward?

A. It looked like that.

Q. All of this testimony is just the best you could do under the adverse circumstances, and you would have no way of knowing if it was shooting, assuming that it was shooting at the *Montebello,* you would have no way of knowing the distance between the submarine and the *Montebello* at the time you saw those flashes?

A. No, I wouldn't know that.

Q. When was it you first attempted to estimate the distance of the flashes from Piedras Blancas, when did you first do that?

A. I think when the matter was first brought up and I was asked to look back and remember such details as I could.

Q. That was a representative of the War Damage Corporation?

A. I believe it was at that time.

Q. Do you recall that after Mr. Charles or Mr. Bartholomew had been up there that Mr. Powell and myself and two naval officers called upon you?

A. Yes.

Q. Do you recall on that occasion we asked you to estimate the distance and you thought you could not do it?

A. I don't remember if I told you at that time, or not; however, 5-miles is what I had estimated it. Did you ask me that?

Q. Yes.

A. If I told you I think five miles, that would have been the answer, approximately.

Q. But you are not sure you told us?

A. Well, I don't remember all the details.

Q. Do you recall Mr. Urick, a representative from my office, coming to see you about two weeks ago and you refused to talk to him?

A. Yes, because I had said everything I knew about the matter; I had nothing further to talk about.

Mr. Sandmeyer: That is all.

Courtroom Testimony:
Paul Sandmeyer questioning Olof Ekstrom

Shortly afterwards I passed Estero Bay—that is the bay you see on the coast—the Standard Oil Company have a loading station there at that point—an hour and a half after I passed Point Buchon. I saw some gun flashes on my starboard quarter, and at that time I increased the speed. I realized there was some enemy surface vessel or submarine in that vicinity.

Shortly afterwards I received a message from the Navy Department that a submarine or surface vessel was shelling a tanker by the name of the *Larry Doheny*. I again increased the speed. There was no chance to go back. The submarine was behind me. So I had to keep going ahead. And at about 5:30 or so in the morning, still darkness, some of the men discovered what appeared to be a submarine. It was on the surface behind. There was identification of a submarine there. I again asked for more speed and to head in toward shore, to get in as close to the beach as possible, since there was a possibility that the submarine would not be able to get into shallow water. I was not so much afraid at that time of being torpedoed, but more afraid of gunfire. We were loaded with crude oil, which is quite explosive. I was afraid of fire.

Well, I was zigzagging toward shore, maybe right and left, left and right. I don't recall, because everything was in confusion. You don't have much time.

Fifteen minutes afterwards I felt a terrific concussion. The ship was vibrating. Everything came down, including myself, and I knew then we were torpedoed. I never saw the torpedo coming, but some men saw the torpedo in the water. The telegraph, the radio, the telephone—everything went down under water due to the explosion. The ship—she was it somewhere on the forepart, on the starboard, the right side. To my belief she still had a speed on her, making about 11 knots or 11 miles per hour. I don't know for sure if the engine was stopped at that moment, or it was stopped later, but the lights were off, the dynamos went off—everything was just a confusion. I told the radio operator over the speaking tube to send in an S.O.S. He informed me his radio set had already come down. I told him to use the emergency set and he informed me that that also was down.

I ordered them to get the boats ready and get off the ship, and then I tried to ascertain the extent of the damage. It was settled down quite a bit by the head—I mean she went down this way and the stern came up. The after end came up. And I looked at the 'tween-deck in the forehold and I only heard a lot of noise, oil running out and water running in, and vice-versa, and I was afraid of fire. You could still smell the powder burning, the oakite from the TNT.

I proceeded to my room to open the safe and get the ship's papers and the money out, and in the darkness—I had no light and I wasn't able to open the combination. I grabbed a life preserver in that vicinity and I went back aft. We had four lifeboats and all four lifeboats were placed on the after end of the vessel. We had no boats 'tween ships. I went back there and told the men, "Don't be excited. Take it easy." The ship wasn't going to sink right away.

Just when I said that, the submarine was on the surface and began to shell us. Of course, then it made a little more confusion. Eventually I got three boats out in the water. I accounted for all the men. On one boat were ten men, on two boats were eleven men each. I had another lifeboat, No.1 on the starboard side. There were six of us left on the ship, so we got the boat ready, down in the water. She started to sink. I slipped down on the boat fall. We cut the painter, what held the ship fast or what held the boat, what tied the boat up to the ship, and then I slid astern of the vessel, and came around this way (indicating). When I got into the boat I discovered the boat was full of water. I didn't realize why it was full of water. We laid around while they shelled us with 4-inch shells.

Mr. Charles: If the court please, I am sorry to interrupt, but I overlooked asking your Honor to make the usual order to exclude witnesses who have any knowledge of the facts of the case from the courtroom, and may I ask your Honor to make such an order at the present time?

The Court: Any witnesses who have been subpoenaed and called here will retire to the witness room just outside the courtroom until called. They may be excused from the courtroom, any witnesses who have been called.

Mr. Sandmeyer: That includes the defendant's witnesses, as well.

The Court: Both sides. Proceed.

The Witness: When we got the boat clear of the ship's side, I pulled the boat around the stern, and at that time it appeared to me that the vessel was heading in a southwesterly direction, or the stern was in towards Piedras Blancas Light, and the bow was heading a little bit out in a southwesterly direction from Piedras Blancas Light. I then pulled away from the ship, about 500 feet away from the vessel until she sank, and when she went down it was exactly approximately 55 minutes to an hour from the time she was hit with the torpedo until she was definitely submerged.

I believe the vessel went down, checking on the course and speed, at least when she was hit she was approximately a mile and a half to two miles from the shoreline, to my best recollection. I cannot recall absolutely where it happened because we had no timer to take bearings and check anything. Time has gone by since that time and I don't recall for sure, but we took and we pulled the boat—I would say the boat was waterlogged, and we finally landed—my boat landed on the beach amongst the rocks.

I was thrown overboard from the boat when we reached the rocks. It was full of oil from the fuel oil, crude oil. The boat was so slippery, and I had a steering oar standing aft of the boat, and when the boat hit the rocks I was thrown overboard and was carried out to sea. I was later on rescued by some people ashore, who came there—the fire department and some policemen, farmers, and I don't know who else. There was a bunch on the rocks around there waiting to give us a hand. According to my figures, the distance, from the time we left the vessel until we landed and the boat was water-logged, it couldn't have been much more than two miles from the shore.

Q. Captain Ekstrom, when you sighted the submarine shortly after, did you send any radio message, whatever?

A. I sent in a radio message that a surface vessel or submarine tried to attack four miles southwest of Piedras Blancas, or south— I don't recall, either south or southwest of Piedras Blancas.

Q. How long a time, in your estimate, passed between the

time you saw the submarine until the torpedo struck, that is, the explosion?

A. Approximately ten or fifteen minutes.

Q. When you saw the submarine, did I understand you to testify that you gave some order with reference to speed?

A. When I sighted the submarine, I do not recall if I gave them…

Q. Captain, when the vessel was sunk, I believe you said it went down by the bow first. I wonder if you could describe to the jury how the vessel sank?

A. When the vessel was torpedoed she settled down almost immediately on the fore part, and then she settled gradually more and more, and by the time she went down, the after end of the vessel came up about 150 feet in the air, and then she went straight down.

Q. That is, the after end of the vessel was vertical to the surface of the water and she went straight down?

A. She went straight down.

Q. You saw her stern go up in the air, did you?

A. I did, yes, sir.

Q. I believe you said you were about 500 feet away, or 500 yards?

A. Approximately five or six hundred feet away.

Q. Did I understand you to say this morning that the distance where she sunk was a mile and a half to two miles from the shoreline?

A. Approximately. It might have been more, it might have been less.

Q. That would be approximately where this Point H is (indicating)?

A. Approximately. She was torpedoed at Point H.

Q. Could you tell us about how near that point she sank?

A. I wouldn't know for absolutely sure how close she was to that point. It might have been a mile or so either way.

Q. It might have been what?

A. It might have been a mile or a half-mile from that point.

[Cross examination.[

Mr. Charles: Q. ... [omitted] circulated among the Navy and that there is a statement in that wreck list that the position of the wreck is given so that the vessels of the United States won't be depth bombing their own wrecks?

A. That position on the chart where the ship went down is placed approximately. If you take a chart of the Atlantic Coast, a wreck chart where thousands of ships were torpedoed on the Atlantic Coast during this war, there isn't one in the correct position.

Q. I do not want to argue with you on that. There probably isn't one of them that was torpedoed just a few miles from her port of departure. What I am asking—and I don't want to quarrel with you—is just this thing: You do know, don't you, that the location of the wreck of a ship in time of war, when our vessels are looking for an enemy submarine, is and was of vital importance?

A. The Navy Intelligence and the Army Intelligence no doubt know where the vessel was.

Q. Why would they know where it was other than from your testimony?

A. At that time when the vessel was sunk we was at war and everything was a military secret. There was no person outside of myself that was supposed to know where that vessel was. That was a military secret. It wasn't supposed it be given out. The Navy and Army Intelligence—it was their business to know exactly if that vessel was a menace to navigation, which they probably did know two hours after the vessel went down.

Q. Captain, I wasn't asking you about a danger to navigation. I was asking you if you did not realize the importance of the position with respect to the danger that the ship would be depth bombed under the misbelief that it was as enemy craft, an enemy submarine?

A. You couldn't depth bomb that thing, because there was no sound from it.

Q. You are familiar with the fact that her wreck list position...

A. I am familiar with submarines; they never depth bomb wrecks.

Q. And also there is an explicit direction in the wreck list to use care, or a definite statement in the wreck list that the place of these wrecks is given so that the navy will not be led astray in the bombing of their own wrecks in the belief that they are submarines?

A. It can't be done. Why should we bomb our own wrecks? They are submerged, no noise, and no way to detect.

Q. I will get that wreck list statement and show it to you, Captain. At the time that you made that statement, "4 miles off," you believed it to be correct, didn't you?

A. As far as I did, yes.

End Notes

[1] The Type-95 torpedo was the submarine version of the larger Japanese "Long Lance" Type-93 torpedo fired from surface vessels. It was designed to be launched from the standard twenty-one-inch diameter submarine tube.

[2] A single barrel of crude oil is the equivalent of forty-two gallons. Modern oil tankers now are routinely 1500 feet in length and carry two million barrels of oil. The largest tankers today, the ultra-large crude carrier, have a capacity up to three million barrels.

[3] Oil had been discovered in the Kern River Oil Field in 1899 at a depth of 70-feet.

[4] An Ordinary Seaman is an apprentice to become an Able Seaman and is usually an individual with one to two years of experience aboard ship.

5. The Type-95 torpedo, a modification of the devastating "Long Lance" Type-93 torpedo used by Japanese surface vessels, was technologically sophisticated, carried a huge warhead, and was the fastest torpedo in use by any navy of the time. At a distance of 10,000 yards the Type-95 maintained a speed of 50 knots. As impressive as its capabilities were, Captain Tameichi Hara of the Imperial Japanese Navy noted one shortcoming of the torpedo: they were so sensitive, he said, they occasionally detonated "when they hit turbulent water, such as the wake of a ship."

6. Ekstrom would later testify he thought the time of the explosions to be near 4:20 AM. This, however, is inconsistent with both the reports from the Cayucos residents and radio operator William Barnhart's testimony he had received the message of the Larry Doheny attack near 3:00 AM.

7. Names vary regarding who first sighted the submarine. But there is no dispute that Quincy (age 22), McLean (age 48), and Frez (age 23), were the observers who steadily conveyed the submarine's relative position to Ekstrom as the Montebello began zigzagging.

8. It was later determined the torpedo struck forward of the oil tanks in the pump room and dry-storage area—between the oil tanks and the bow.

9. The ranch, consisting of close to six thousand acres, was part of the original Asuncion Rancho (nearly forty thousand acres). Harper Sibley purchased the ranch property in 1929. Sibley was a prominent national figure—once president of the United States Chamber of Commerce—with vast farm holdings in Illinois, mining interests in West Virginia, timber on the West Coast, and ranchlands in High River, Alberta, Canada. His grandfather, Hiram Sibley, was a founder and first president of Western Union Telegraph Company. Hiram, like his grandson, had also invested

successfully in land, timber, coal, and railroads.

[10.] The *I-21's* lone goal in the attack was to sink the Montebello. In the rolling seas and darkness of that morning, a competent sub commander would never risk his own crew's safety—on a wet and pitching deck, no less—for an irrelevant purpose. None of the men in other lifeboats reported being fired upon by a machine gun. Further, Frez was in the same lifeboat as Ekstrom, and the captain made no mention—ever—of a machine-gun attack on his crew, including in his extensive 1946 courtroom testimony.

[11.] Fayette Dow was general counsel of the National Petroleum Association in Washington, D.C.

[12.] Jesse Jones was chairman of the RFC—concurrent with his position as the United States Secretary of Commerce. PBS's "Brother, Can You Spare a Billion?" story on Jones stated he "directed billions of dollars toward needy banks, industries, farmers and citizens, making him arguably the most powerful man in the world financial community," prompting Franklin Roosevelt to sometimes refer to him as "Jesus Jones."

[13.] Ewing worked at Woods Hole before and during his undergraduate days at Harvard. He would later become the chairman of the Department of Geology and Geophysics at WHOI.

[14.] Fifty years later, Dr. John Ewing, in an interview, said, "We got pictures of the ship, and we got it accurately located. It was over three miles [off the coast]. The complainers said, 'Well, okay, it's there now; but it slid down [laughter] and came to rest where it is.' Fran and I manned echo sounders and stitched the thing in pretty well and for that to have happened, the ship would have had to go down to the bottom and then come up over quite a nice ridge and then go down the other side. [Laughter]"

Index

Artillery range, 51
Astoria, Oregon, 60
Atlantic Coast, 108
Atlantic Ocean, 14, 21
Australia, 74, 129
Avila
    Customs House, 29, 30, 67
    Front Street, 28, 68, 130, 131
    occupations, 27
    pier, 28, 30, 31
    post-war history, 130
    storage tanks, 28, 30, 130
    town of, 27-32, 65-68
Avila Alliance, 130
Avila Beach, 130
Avila Fountain, 28, 32
Avila Grocery, 28-29, 131

Balboa, Canal Zone, 22
Baltic Sea, 42
Baltimore Sun, 88
Barnhart, William, 70, 72
Beggiatoa bacteria, 122
Belgium, 49
Big Sur, 46
Blackouts, 15
Blakeslee, Sam, 122
Bodega Bay, 120
Bohemian immigrants, 42
Brainerd, William, 97
Breiland, O.S., 57
British Columbia, 21, 40, 51, 93
British Commonwealth, 51
British Expeditionary Force, 49
British scientists, 24

To contact the author: mcdowellsinpg@yahoo.com

Made in the USA
Las Vegas, NV
10 August 2021